Christian Hedonism?

A biblical examination of

John Piper's teaching

E S Williams

Belmont House Publishing

London

Christian Hedonism?

A biblical examination of John Piper's teaching

published by Belmont House Publishing, London

First published September 2017

ISBN 978-0-9954845-1-1

Scripture quotations from Authorised King James Version of the Holy Bible.

Desiring God quotes from the 2011 edition.

The Dangerous Duty of Delight quotes from 2001 edition.

Published by Belmont House Publishing
36 The Crescent
Belmont
SUTTON
Surrey SM2 6BJ

Website www.belmonthouse.co.uk

A Catalogue record for this book is available from the British Library.

Three Youtube videos on John Piper's ministry are available for viewing on the New Calvinist website: www.newcalvinist.com/
> *John Piper in the Dark*
> *Piper's Journey into Hedonism*
> *Folly of Christian Hedonism*

My grateful thanks to the brothers and sisters in Christ, both in the UK and USA, who commented on the manuscript and helped with proof-reading.

Table of Contents

Foreword

The term 'Christian Hedonism' was first coined by Dr. John Piper in his 1986 book *Desiring God*. He summarises this philosophy of the Christian life as, 'God is most glorified in us when we are most satisfied in Him.' Since then his teaching has gathered a huge following, not only in the USA but farther afield, including the UK.

According to Piper it was his 'persistent and undeniable yearning for happiness' that led to his formulating Christian Hedonism. Taking this as his starting-point, Piper makes Scripture (wrenched from its context) reflect this teaching, and claims the writings of Jonathan Edwards to support this view of Christian experience. Piper even confesses himself influenced by other men not known for their orthodoxy: Daniel Fuller, Blaise Pascal, and C.S. Lewis. The writings of the latter two have particularly helped shape his novel doctrine of Christian Hedonism.

Unsound doctrine always leads to unsound practice, and it is not surprising that Piper is a leading spokesman for the New Calvinists and a prominent speaker at young people's Passion Conferences, which are characterised by a rock-concert atmosphere and sensual worship. Here, Piper can be heard articulating his Christian Hedonism, devoid of any call to repentance or to saving faith in Jesus Christ.* Unregenerate young people can embrace this hedonism and still be strangers to the Christ 'Who gave himself for our sins, that he might deliver us from this present evil world, according to the will of God and our Father' (Galatians 1.4).

God's worship suffers when there is deviation from Scripture, and Piper's teaching is no exception. It is good, therefore, to have chapter 5 devoted to this subject, which shows what happens to worship when Christian Hedonism is followed, and what is true and scriptural worship. Also, chapter 4 on 'Love' shows how this divine attribute is seriously misrepresented, and what Scripture really teaches on this precious subject.

We are indebted to Ted Williams for this discerning and probing analysis of Christian Hedonism, which proves that, far from it being scriptural and to the glory of God, it is instead unscriptural and man-centred. It is leading many astray in these confused days, appealing as it does to fleshly self-interest and a religion devoid of discipleship, self-denial, and genuine joy in God.

What impresses us in this book is the thoroughness and fairness of its treatment. The copious endnotes and many Scripture references show that Dr. Williams has examined this teaching with painstaking care. He analyses all the key Scriptures, together with the relevant parts of the Westminster Confession of Faith, to show the falsity of Piper's teaching. He shows that Christian Hedonism is a departure from biblical and historic Christianity, and a dangerous error.

To those who have accepted this Christian philosophy as orthodox, as well as those who are confused or uncertain about it, I warmly commend this book. Read it prayerfully with an open Bible, and under God's blessing it will help establish you in the truth of genuine Christian experience and in the right ways of the Lord.

John P. Thackway
Pastor of Holywell Evangelical Church, North Wales, and editor of the *Bible League Quarterly*.

* See Dr. Williams' DVD 'John Piper in the Dark'. Available from: http://www.newcalvinist.com/john-piper-dark-passion/

Introduction

What are we to make of John Piper? Impeccably Reformed and Bible-believing, passionate, articulate, highly intelligent... and yet... and yet many Bible-believing Christians feel uneasy about his radical message of Christian Hedonism. It just does not seem quite right to link the two words, *Christian* and *Hedonism*. There seems to be something wrong somewhere, but what is it?

Since 1986, when his now famous book, *Desiring God*, first burst upon the scene, this Reformed Baptist pastor and theologian from America has preached and taught his new doctrine of Christian Hedonism across the world, winning over many, especially many young people, to his radical new view of the Christian Faith.

This short book seeks to explain what is actually wrong with Christian Hedonism and John Piper's ministry. If it were simply another case of over-emphasising one aspect of the spiritual life and making it the key to sanctification, he would not be the first well-meaning pastor to make that mistake. We believe Piper's error is far more serious than that. We argue that Christian Hedonism is an insidiously destructive system of false teaching that wrecks the authentic Christian life and shamefully distorts the Word of God.

These are the most serious charges to bring against a Christian teacher. Can they be sustained? We trust this carefully researched and well referenced book does just that—sustain our charges against both Christian Hedonism and John Piper's ministry.

Chapter 1

A Flawed Foundation

John Piper is perhaps the most well known and the most popular preacher in the USA at the present day. His charismatic personality and powerful, persuasive preaching style have made him extremely influential among young evangelical Christians both within and beyond America. His new and radical doctrine of Christian Hedonism is becoming increasingly fashionable, especially among the younger generation. In *For the Fame of God's Name: Essays in Honor of John Piper* (2010), David Wells, Research Professor of Gordon Conwell Theological Seminary, Massachusetts, writes: 'This book is a tribute to one of the extraordinary pastors of our generation, who in many ways broke the mold. He has big thoughts about God in a time when God and his glory have been much diminished in the church. His has been a God-centered ministry.'[1] Mark Noll, Professor of History at University of Notre Dame, Indiana, is equally effusive in his praise. He comments: 'Its authors offer the best sort of tribute by seriously engaging the Scriptures to which Piper is committed, earnestly expounding the classic Calvinistic doctrines into which Piper has breathed such life, and zealously promoting the glory of God to which Piper has devoted his ministry.'[2]

Piper has the reputation of being a five-point Calvinist. On his Desiring God website he affirms: 'I begin as a Bible-believing Christian who wants to put the Bible above all systems of thought. But over the years – many years of struggle – I have deepened in my conviction that Calvinistic teachings on the five points are biblical and therefore true, and therefore a precious pathway into deeper experiences of God's grace.'[3]

Despite his massive popularity and his reputation as a sound theologian and Bible scholar, many believe that Piper is actually compromising the Reformed faith that he claims to preach and teach. In this book we examine Piper's doctrine of Christian Hedonism and reveal a number of deeply disturbing errors. While many will have difficulty in accepting that there are problems with Piper's ministry, we ask readers to patiently and soberly consider the carefully documented evidence presented here in the light of biblical truth.

A flawed foundation

As we start our evaluation of Piper's ministry, we need to recognise the formative influence of three men who helped him formulate the concept of Christian Hedonism: the leading new-evangelical American academic Daniel Fuller, Dean of Fuller Theological Seminary in the USA; the French Roman Catholic religious philosopher and mathematician Blaise Pascal; and the famous British Anglo-Catholic academic and religious author, C.S. Lewis. All this intellectual stimulation undoubtedly helped to develop the ideas that culminated in the publication in 1986 of the best-selling book, *Desiring God.* It had an immediate and far-reaching impact, and began Piper's long ministry as the promoter of Christian Hedonism. Such was the impact of this book that four further editions have followed, the latest in 2016.

Daniel Fuller – partial inspiration of Scripture

On the Desiring God website Piper explains the great influence of Daniel Fuller on his understanding of the Christian Faith. He writes: 'My love for Daniel Fuller is unashamed. I owe him more than I can describe.'[4] Piper openly acknowledges the influence of Fuller Seminary on his theological thinking. In 1967, Daniel Fuller delivered a paper before the Evangelical Theological Society of America wherein he laid the groundwork for what may be called a doctrine of 'partial inspiration'.[5] By the end of the 1960s, Fuller Seminary's view of Scripture was seriously compromised; 'limited inerrancy' was the dominant view. Fuller argued that there are two kinds of Scripture—revelational Scripture that is wholly without error and non-revelational Scripture that is not without error.[6] Yet Piper happily worked alongside Fuller, and he even wrote the foreword to his book, *The Unity of the Bible* (1992). 'No book besides the Bible has had a greater influence on my life than Daniel Fuller's *The Unity of the Bible*. When I first read it as a classroom syllabus over twenty years ago, everything began to change.'[7] Piper continued his endorsement with these words: 'This book will be of immense value to the Church. It will be useful in seminaries, colleges, and Bible schools where teachers and students struggle to see the Bible as a whole... But not only there, the book will also serve the local church in classes and small study groups...'[8] So he enthusiastically promoted a book by a man who did not hold to the inerrancy of Scripture. Undoubtedly, Piper is the product of Fuller Seminary's liberal, compromised view of the Christian Faith.

Blaise Pascal – human philosophy

Piper's system of Christian Hedonism had its roots in the thinking of the 17th-century religious philosopher Blaise Pascal. Piper writes: 'During my first quarter in seminary I was introduced to the argument for Christian Hedonism and one of its great exponents, Blaise Pascal.'[9] Piper eagerly accepted Pascal's assertion that all men, without exception, seek happiness. To develop his construct of Christian Hedonism, all he then had to do was scan the Scriptures to find biblical verses that appeared to support Pascal's theory. But in so doing he committed a cardinal error, for he started with the ideas of men, and then turned to Scripture to justify a human philosophical system. But this is the wrong way round; this is not how Scripture should be used. Sound Christian thinking always starts with God's Word, not with man's word. 'Thus saith the Lord, Cursed be the man that trusteth in man, and maketh flesh his arm, and whose heart departeth from the LORD' (Jeremiah 17.5).

C.S. Lewis – unorthodox apologist

While in college, Piper grew to love the work of C.S. Lewis. In 1964, when he started his studies at Wheaton College, he was introduced to Lewis's *Mere Christianity*. He writes: 'For the next five or six years I was almost never without a Lewis book near at hand. I think without his influence I would never have lived my life with as much joy and usefulness as I have... I will never cease to thank God for this remarkable man who came onto my path at the perfect moment.'[10] But it was some years later, in 1986, that he came across Lewis's sermon, 'The Weight of Glory', which had a profound influence on his thinking. 'I had never in my whole life heard any Christian, let alone a Christian of Lewis's stature, say that all of us not only seek (as Pascal said) but also *ought to seek* our own happiness'[11] (emphasis in original).

But C.S. Lewis was not a sound guide, for he had a confused understanding of the Christian Faith. In particular, his view of the Bible was unorthodox. He certainly did not believe in the inerrancy of Scripture. Philip Ryken, President of Wheaton College in the USA, in a lecture entitled, 'Inerrancy and the Patron Saint of Evangelicalism: C.S. Lewis on Holy Scripture', highlights three of Lewis's shortcomings. 'C.S. Lewis placed the inspiration of Scripture on a continuum with other forms of literary inspiration, thus downplaying to some degree the uniqueness of the Bible… A second shortcoming in Lewis's doctrine of Scripture is that he believed there were contradictions and probably errors in the Bible… A third shortcoming is closely related to the second: C.S. Lewis doubted or denied that certain parts of the Bible were historical, including books that evangelicals traditionally have regarded as historical narrative.' Ryken makes the point that 'Lewis comes perilously close to a neo-orthodox view of Scripture, in which the biblical text is not inherently divine but only becomes the Word of God when the Spirit of God makes it so for the reader.'[12]

Theologian John W. Robbins, founder of The Trinity Foundation in the USA, having analysed the writings of C.S. Lewis in some detail, reached the following conclusion: 'Lewis taught and believed in purgatory (despite the fact that Article 22 of the Thirty-nine Articles of the Church of England describes the doctrine of purgatory as "repugnant to the Word of God"), said prayers for the dead, believed in the physical presence of Christ's body and blood in the bread and wine, a sacrament that he came to call "Mass", practiced and taught auricular confession, believed in baptismal salvation, and free will. As we have seen, he rejected the inerrancy of Scripture and justification by faith alone, as well as the doctrines of total depravity and the sovereignty of God.'[13] Lewis remained an Anglo-Catholic all his life and had a close association with the eminent Roman Catholic authors J.R.R. Tolkien and G.K. Chesterton, who undoubtedly had a large influence on his theological thinking. Clearly, then, during his theological training, Piper subjected himself to unorthodox and misleading influences.

Endnotes

1   *For the Fame of God's Name: Essays in Honor of John Piper*, edited by Sam Storms and Justin Taylor, Crossway, 2010, back page blurb

2   Ibid.

3   Desiring God website, article by John Piper, 'What We Believe About the Five Points of Calvinism', March 1985, http://www.desiringgod.org/articles/what-we-believe-about-the-five-points-of-calvinism

4   Desiring God website, article by John Piper, 'Praise God for Fundamentalists', October 31, 2007, http://www.desiringgod.org/articles/praise-god-for-fundamentalists

5   Evangelical Reformed Fellowship Website, 'The Necessary Consonance of the Doctrines of Scripture: Inspiration, Inerrancy, and Authority' by Steve Curtis http://evangelicalreformedfellowship.org/InspirationandInerr.aspx.

6   Harold Lindsell, *The Battle for the Bible*, Zondervan, 1981, p113

7   Daniel Fuller, *The Unity of the Bible*, 1992, Foreword by John Piper, page x

8   Ibid, p xii

9   John Piper, *Desiring God*, Multinomah, 2011, p19

10   John Piper, *Don't Waste your Life*, Christ Is All Media Publications, 2003, pp19-20

11   *Desiring God*, p20

12   Desiring God website, 'Inerrancy and the Patron Saint of Evangelicalism: C.S. Lewis on Holy Scripture', Plenary 2 — 2013 National Conference, 'The Romantic Rationalist: God, Life, and Imagination in the Work of C.S. Lewis', message by Philip Ryken

13   Trinity Foundation website, 'Did C.S. Lewis Go to Heaven?', John W. Robbins http://www.trinityfoundation.org/journal.php?id=103

Chapter 2

Piper's Journey into Christian Hedonism

In *Don't Waste Your Life* (2003), John Piper describes how C.S. Lewis 'walked up over the horizon of my little brown path in 1964 with such blazing brightness that it is hard to overstate the impact he had on my life. Someone introduced me to Lewis in my freshman year with the book *Mere Christianity*... He demonstrated for me and convinced me that rigorous, precise, penetrating logic is not opposed to deep, soul-stirring feeling and vivid, lively – even playful – imagination... Lewis gave me an intense sense of the "realness" of things... He helped me become alive to life.'[1]

As noted in chapter 1, at Fuller Theological Seminary Piper came under the influence of new evangelical Daniel Fuller. Piper writes: 'My debt at this point to Daniel Fuller is incalculable. He taught me hermeneutics—the science of how to interpret the Bible... What a gift those three years of seminary were! In the final class with Dr Fuller, called "The Unity of the Bible", the unifying flag was hoisted over the whole Bible.'[2] Piper explains how the seeds of his life were rooted in Daniel Fuller's book, *The Unity of the Bible*. 'One of the seeds was in the word "glory"—God's aim in history was to "fully display his glory". Another seed was in the word "delight"—God's aim was that his people "delight in him with all their hearts". The passage of my life has been to understand and live and teach and preach how these two aims of God relate to each other—indeed, how they are not two but one.' Piper goes on: 'If my life was to have a single, all-satisfying, unifying passion, it would have to be God's passion. And, if Daniel Fuller was right, God's passion was the display of his own glory and the delight of my heart... Enjoying God supremely is one way to glorify him. Enjoying God makes him look supremely valuable.'[3]

Piper freely acknowledges that the foundation of Christian Hedonism was laid at Fuller Theological Seminary. While the words *glory, delight, enjoying* were firmly implanted in the young Piper's mind, the concept of *obedience* to God's law is not mentioned.

In *Desiring God*, Piper explains his conversion to Christian Hedonism in this way. During his first quarter in seminary, he came across the writings of Blaise Pascal, who had written, 'All men seek happiness. This is without exception.' Piper was enthralled: 'This statement so fit with my own deep longings… that I accepted it and have never found any reason to doubt it.'[4] Having uncritically accepted Pascal's philosophy, he accepted also the proposition that God made man to desire pleasure—'seeking one's own happiness is not sin; it is a simple given in human nature'.[5] Piper explains: 'I found in myself an overwhelming longing to be happy, a tremendously powerful impulse to seek pleasure, yet at every point of moral decision I said to myself that this impulse should have no influence… Then I was converted to Christian Hedonism. In a matter of weeks I came to see that it is unbiblical and arrogant to try to worship God for any other reason than the pleasure to be had in Him.'[6] *So, it is about getting pleasure for ourselves*

As we saw in chapter 1, in 1986 Piper discovered the sermon, 'The Weight of Glory', in which C.S. Lewis says Christians ought to seek their own happiness. He was overjoyed, for it seemed to confirm all he had read in Pascal, and so he wrote: 'As I look back on it now, it seems so patently obvious that I don't know how I could have missed it. All those years I had been trying to suppress my tremendous longing for happiness… But now it started to dawn on me that this persistent and undeniable yearning for happiness was not to be suppressed, but to be glutted—on God!' Lewis had helped to convince him that 'praise should be motivated solely by the happiness we find in God…'[7]

With the concept of Christian Hedonism firmly implanted in his mind, Piper turned to the Psalms and says he 'found the language of Hedonism everywhere. The quest for pleasure was not even optional, but *commanded*: "Delight yourself in the LORD, and he will give you the desires of your heart" (Psalm 37.4)'[8] (my emphasis). The important point to note is that he only found 'the language of Hedonism everywhere' in the Bible *after* he had been influenced by the ideas of Pascal and Lewis. In other words, he was now reading the Bible through the lens of Christian Hedonism.

And so Piper went on to develop a new philosophy of life, which he calls 'Christian Hedonism', based largely on the ideas of Blaise Pascal and C.S. Lewis. He explains: 'My shortest summary of it is: God is most glorified in us when we are most satisfied in him. Or: The chief end of man is to glorify God *by* enjoying him forever.'[9] Piper's study of human philosophy, masquerading as profound spiritual insight, convinced him that all decisions and conduct in life are predicated on man's innate desire to find pleasure. And, of course, those who dedicate their lives to the pursuit of pleasure have been known throughout the ages as *hedonists*, a word which has always carried a pejorative connotation. So his flawed approach to theology allowed him to integrate human philosophy with the Christian Faith, and the result was Christian Hedonism and the Desiring God ministry.

Spokesman for the New Calvinism

Piper stands at the very centre of the so-called New Calvinism movement and is widely regarded as its chief spokesman. In March 2014, he delivered a lecture at Westminster Seminary, Philadelphia, on the subject: 'The New Calvinism and the New Community: The Doctrines of Grace and the Meaning of Race'.[10] He explained his role: 'I am part of the New Calvinism and feel a sense of fatherly responsibility to continually speak into it dimensions of biblical truth that I think it needs to hear.' He defined his understanding of New Calvinism, and then offered twelve defining features of the movement, stressing that the characteristics of New Calvinism did not necessarily separate it from traditional Calvinism or make the new better than the old.

His first point was that New Calvinism, in its allegiance to the inerrancy of the Bible, embraced the biblical truths behind the five points of Calvinism (TULIP). He said that 'The New Calvinism has a strong complementarian flavor with an emphasis on the flourishing of men and women in relationships where men embrace the call to robust, humble, Christ-like, servant leadership.'

He noted that the New Calvinism movement included both charismatics and non-charismatics. He observed that it is energetically

9

engaged in publishing books, and in using the Internet, with hundreds of bloggers and social media activists spreading the message. He ended by claiming that New Calvinism is robustly gospel-centred. Significantly, Piper did not mention New Calvinism's devotion to contemporary Christian worship, and its association with Christian 'rap' and 'holy hip-hop'.

Desiring God ministry

Over the last three decades Piper's Desiring God ministry and website has focused on the doctrine of Christian Hedonism, a term first used in the first edition of his famous book, *Desiring God*, in 1986. Since the publication of *Desiring God*, Piper has taken every opportunity to promote his philosophy through numerous sermons, books, articles, YouTube videos and conference addresses in the USA and across the world. In 2001 he published a summary of his philosophical system in the book, *The Dangerous Duty of Delight*. There is little doubt that Piper's name will forever be associated with the philosophy of Christian Hedonism—a concept which he regards as the central organising principle of the Christian life, the single most important spiritual duty of all born-again Christians. He teaches that God's greatest commandment is 'Delight yourself in the Lord', from Psalm 37.4. Christian Hedonism has had an enormous and continuing impact, particularly upon the young. Piper defines hedonism as a devotion to pleasure as a way of life. From this spiritual starting point, Piper's philosophy has become a global ministry.

The Passion movement

The importance of the annual Passion Conference in Atlanta, Georgia, as a platform for Christian Hedonism, can hardly be exaggerated. The stated purpose of the Passion movement, founded by Louis Giglio in 1997, is to unite students 'in worship and prayer for spiritual awakening in this generation'. The theme verse is Isaiah 26.8: 'Your name and renown are the desire of our souls'. Giglio's vision is for each rising generation of young people, aged between 18 and 25, to hear about Jesus in a culturally appropriate context; hence the rock-concert atmosphere of large Passion gatherings. Piper has been the keynote speaker at the annual Passion Conference on numerous occasions, delivering seventeen messages to date.[11]

The focus of Piper's first Passion address in 1997 was Christian Hedonism. Preaching to a large audience of young people, he declared: 'So my call to you now, in the name of God Almighty, is that you might make it your eternal vocation to pursue your pleasure with all the might that God mightily inspires within you.'[12] Over the years, through these Passion gatherings, Piper has sought to persuade hundreds of thousands of young people to follow the way of Christian Hedonism.

The future of Christian Hedonism

In October 2016 Piper preached a sermon entitled, 'Fifteen Dreams for the Future of Christian Hedonism', at the Indulge seminar, hosted by Bethlehem College & Seminary in Minneapolis, attached to his own Bethlehem Baptist Church.[13]

He began this sermon by describing the heart of Christian Hedonism as, 'Not just the permission, but the duty – the obligation – to pursue the maximum enjoyment of God.' He offered the following definition of Christian Hedonism:

'Since God is most glorified in us when we are most satisfied in him, therefore, in everything we do, we should always be pursuing maximum satisfaction in God and striving to take as many people with us into that satisfaction as we can, even if it costs us our lives.'

He went on to explain his understanding of the word hedonism: 'My old *Webster's Collegiate Dictionary* of 1961 defines hedonism as "a living for pleasure." And the *American Heritage Dictionary of the English Language*, fourth edition, has as its first definition: "pursuit of or devotion to pleasure." And www.dictionary.com gives as its second definition, "devotion to pleasure as a way of life." That is precisely what I mean by the term. And I insist upon the radical position that the only pleasures that oblige us to seek them – the only ones morally obligated by God – are ones that you cannot feel unless you are born again—spiritual pleasures made possible by the creation of a new heart.'

Piper referred to the Westminster Shorter Catechism: 'It seems to me that anyone who agrees with the Westminster Catechism that "Man's chief end is to glorify God and enjoy God forever," would have to agree that this enjoyment of God can be nothing less than an *ultimate duty* [emphasis added]. That is, we are duty-bound to pursue maximum pleasure in God. Christian Hedonism says that this is not optional. It is at the heart of what it means to be a Christian—to be saved. Christian Hedonism goes so far as to say that if you don't pursue your maximum pleasure in God, you can neither worship God nor love people. In other words, essential to God-glorifying worship is the experience of God as your greatest treasure and most satisfying pleasure.'[14]

Piper is so convinced of his doctrine of Christian Hedonism that in the above quote he has boldly asserted that unless we follow it, we are not able to worship God or even love people! A careful evaluation of this sermon raises the very disturbing thought: Is Piper, by his persuasive oratory, attempting to turn the Christian Faith into a worldwide hedonistic cult? Yes

Piper's commandment

In the preface to *Desiring God*, Piper asserts: 'This is a serious book about being happy in God. It's about happiness because that is what our Creator commands: "Delight yourself in the LORD" (Psalm 37.4). And it is serious because, as Jeremy Taylor [the celebrated 17th-century High Church Anglican divine] said, "God threatens terrible things if we will not be happy".'[15] Piper has used this phrase from Psalm 37.4 to create a new commandment for the Christian Church. He refers to this verse 10 times in *Desiring God* (more than he refers to any other single verse) as he seeks to construct and press home the idea that we are actually *commanded* to 'Delight in the Lord'. Piper's 'delight commandment' has two sides to it—the action of taking pleasure in God, and the threat of punishment if we do not obey the command.

Here are some examples of his reasoning from *Desiring God*. He provides seven reasons why he has written the book, and the third is: 'The Word of God *commands* us to pursue our joy.' He helps to support this assertion by simply quoting, 'Delight yourself in the LORD' (Psalm 37.4).[16] He writes elsewhere: 'I say that God *commands* that we find joy in loving God: "Delight yourself in the LORD" (Psalm 37.4)'[17] He also says, 'The real duty of worship is not the outward duty to say or do the liturgy. It is the inward duty, the *command*: "Delight yourself in the

12

LORD"! (Psalm 37.4)'[18] He says, 'Worship is nothing less than obedience to the *command* of God: "Delight yourself in the LORD"!'[19] He writes: 'Between man and God, on the vertical axis of life, the pursuit of pleasure is not just tolerable; it is *mandatory*: "Delight yourself in the LORD"! (Psalm 37.4)'.[20] (My emphasis throughout.)

Speaking on the subject of Christian Hedonism at the 1997 Passion Conference, Piper commented on Psalm 37.4: 'This is not a suggestion, this is a commandment. If you believe, "Thou shalt not commit adultery" is something you should obey, then you should also obey, "Delight yourself in the LORD".'[21] *not a command. (His opinion)*

There can be little doubt from such statements that he is promulgating a conscience-binding commandment on all Christians. Piper has here equated his own 'delight commandment' with God's Seventh Commandment, implying thereby that they are, in effect, of equal authority! He has taken part of one verse completely out of context and with it created a new commandment.

But Piper is wrong to assert that the phrase quoted from Psalm 37 is a commandment. The law of God was delivered by Moses, not by David. In Psalm 37 David is bearing witness to the goodness and faithfulness of God. The context of the Psalm is that believers should not fear evil men, because God is the deliverer of the righteous. And so David gives several encouraging exhortations: 'Fret not thyself because of evildoers…Trust in the LORD, and do good'; and then the exhortation, 'Delight thyself also in the LORD; and he shall give thee the desires of thine heart. Commit thy way unto the LORD; trust also in him; and he shall bring it to pass' (Psalm 37.1,3,4,5).

Only by reading verse 4 in context is it possible to understand God's intended meaning from Psalm 37. The purpose of the Psalmist is not to issue a commandment, but to exhort believers in times of affliction to trust in the grace and providence of God; although evil men appear to flourish, the Lord will not forsake His saints. Those who understand the goodness and faithfulness of the Lord are here being encouraged to delight in that same goodness and faithfulness. Piper is wrong to insist that this exhortation is a commandment of God. In effect, Piper has made 'Thou shalt delight in the Lord' the Eleventh Commandment. *X* |

Building on his false 'delight commandment', Piper says, 'I am a Christian Hedonist not for any philosophical or theological reason, but because God commands it…'[22] So an essential justification for Piper's Christian Hedonism is the belief that we are *commanded* to seek delight in God. Here we should note the seriousness of attempting to add to the commandments of God: 'Ye shall not add unto the word which I command you, neither shall ye diminish ought from it, that ye may keep the commandments of the LORD your God which I command you' (Deuteronomy 4.2). And further, we should also note that God said this *after* He had revealed the Ten Commandments on Mount Sinai.

wow!

Endnotes

1   *Don't Waste Your Life*, p19

2   Ibid, pp26-28

3   Ibid, p28

4   *Desiring God*, p19

5   Ibid, p19

6   Ibid, p18

7   Ibid, p21

8   Ibid, p23

9   From Desiring God website: 'Christian Hedonism: Forgive the Label, But Don't Miss the Truth' 1995, http://www.desiringgod.org/resource-library/articles/christian-hedonism

10   Desiring God website, message by John Piper, 'The New Calvinism and the New Community: The Doctrines of Grace and the Meaning of Race', March 12, 2014, http://www.desiringgod.org/messages/the-new-calvinism-and-the-new-community

11   Desiring God website, Passion, http://www.desiringgod.org/passion

12   Piper Passion 1997, www.desiringgod.org/messages/passion-for-the-supremacy-of-god-part-2

13   Desiring God website, Piper sermon, 'Fifteen dreams for the Future of Christian Hedonism', October 2016, www.desiringgod.org/messages/fifteen-dreams-for-the-future-of-christian-hedonism

14   Ibid

15   *Desiring God*, p9

16   Ibid, p293

17   Ibid, pp24-25

18   Ibid, p94

19   Ibid, p98

20   Ibid, p111

21   Piper Passion 1997, www.desiringgod.org/messages/passion-for-the-supremacy-of-god-part-2

22   *Desiring God*, p25

Chapter 3

Piper's Antinomianism

John Piper is in the process of subtly introducing a new deviant way of thinking into the Christian Church that many find confusing. This is because few people are aware of his commitment to *antinomianism*. The word *antinomianism* is from the Greek and means 'against the law' (*anti* – against; *nomos* – law). It may briefly be defined as the doctrine that holds that God's moral law is not binding on Christians as a rule of life. An antinomian believes that because a Christian is under grace, he is no longer under God's moral law as expressed in the Ten Commandments.

The Antinomian Controversy

The ideas of antinomianism were present even in the early Church, as some Gnostic heretics believed that freedom from law meant freedom for licence. The modern doctrine of antinomianism grew out of the Lutheran controversies on law and the gospel during the 16th-century. Martin Luther's collaborator, Johann Agricola (1494-1566), taught that Christians are freed by grace from the need to obey the Ten Command-ments; he was one of the first to promote the ideas of antinomianism in the Church. The term 'Antinomian Controversy' refers to the sharp disagreement that arose between Luther and Agricola. Indeed, Luther coined the word 'antinomian' to describe Agricola and his followers. While Agricola was certainly not a libertine, antinomians like him were known to place a great emphasis on 'love' and saw the law as hostile to grace and faith.

Dr Nick Needham, Church historian and pastor, in volume 4 of *2000 Years of Christ's Power* (2016), explains that the controversy had two phases. In the first, the central figure was Johann Agricola. 'Agricola's basic contention was that Law and Gospel are so radically opposed that Christians no longer had any need of the Law to convict them of sin or work repentance in them—the Gospel alone was sufficient to do this.

Agricola was opposed by both Luther and Melanchthon... After Luther's death, Agricola became more outspoken in his views. The second phase of the antinomian controversy... involved the so-called "third use" of the Law... to teach Christians about the holy life they are to live. Some of Agricola's sympathizers now denied the third use of the Law... These theologians argued that the Law had no teaching or guiding function for the Christian. Indwelt by the Holy Spirit, true believers intuitively knew what was right, and spontaneously did it—they had no need of further guidance. Such views met with the same resistance as Agricola's had. The disciples of both Luther and Melanchthon maintained that the Law was necessary as a moral guide in the Christian life, not least to safeguard believers from false, imaginary views of holiness'.[1] The controversy was finally settled by the Formula of Concord in 1577, where to quote Needham again, 'Lutherans would now acknowledge the third use of the Law—its capacity to guide believers in the way of practical holiness.'

In his essay, 'The Antinomian Controversy Rides Again', Gary Jepsen, an evangelical Lutheran theologian, writes: 'From the perspective of Luther, antinomianism arose out of an inadequate reading of the gospels. It was seen as a reading of scripture that missed the Law-Gospel tension, which was so essential to Luther's thought, because it focused only on a watered down sense of the gospel... And so, the real tragedy of antinomianism is that the gospel is ultimately lost. Without a profound sense for "sin, death and the power of the devil", from what does Christ save us? It is little wonder, therefore, that Luther's reaction to antinomianism, with its rejection of the law, was sharp and unyielding. The gospel, in Luther's eyes, was in danger. "If we cast the Law aside," Luther said, "we shall not long retain Christ".'[2]

Piper's interview

An interview recorded in 2010 as part of the 'Ask Pastor John' series of podcasts, reveals much about Piper's thinking that helps us understand where he is coming from. Piper is asked the straightforward question, 'Are Christians under the Ten Commandments?' His response is unequivocal: 'No. The Bible says we're not under the law. I love Romans 7.4-6. By way of analogy, it says that you are married to the law... And then Paul draws the analogy out – a little complex the way he does it – saying that you died to the law. You aren't married anymore; you can have another husband, namely Christ. He's raised from the dead. So, our approach towards ethics is different. We don't ask the question, "Am I under the law?" We are under grace. The law is already fulfilled perfectly by Jesus.'[3] So Piper, the *Reformed* theologian, has openly declared his antinomianism to the Christian world. His new deviant way of thinking is simply the old antinomianism dressed up in the new clothes of Christian Hedonism.

The Westminster Confession of Faith

All the great Reformed Confessions uphold the continued use of God's moral law. The 1647 Westminster Confession of Faith in chapter 19, 'The Law of God', sets forth the classic Reformed view of the law of God, and helps us to appreciate the significance of Piper's position.

Section 1: 'God gave to Adam a law, as a covenant of works, by which he bound him, and all his posterity, to personal, entire, exact, and perpetual obedience; promising life upon the fulfilling, and threatening death upon the breach of it; and endued him with power and ability to keep it.'

In *An Exposition of the Westminster Confession of Faith* (1998 edition), Robert Shaw, a Scottish Presbyterian theologian (1795-1863), explains: 'God having formed man an intelligent creature, and a subject of moral government, he gave him a law for the rule of his conduct. This law was founded in the infinite righteous nature of God, and the moral relations necessarily subsisting between him and man. It was originally written on the heart of man, as he was endowed with such a perfect knowledge of his Maker's will as was sufficient to inform him concerning the whole extent of his duty…'[4]

Section 2: 'This law, after his fall, continued to be a perfect rule of righteousness; and, as such, was delivered by God upon Mount Sinai in ten commandments, and written in two tables; the first four commandments containing our duty towards God, and the other six our duty to man.'

Section 5: 'The moral law doth for ever bind all, as well justified persons as others, to the obedience thereof; and that not only in regard of the matter contained in it, but also in respect of the authority of God, the Creator, who gave it. Neither doth Christ in the gospel any way dissolve, but much strengthen this obligation.'

Section 6: 'Although true believers be not under the law, as a covenant of works, to be thereby justified, or condemned; yet is it of great use to them, as well as to others; in that, as a rule of life informing them of the will of God, and their duty, it directs and binds them to walk accordingly; discovering also the sinful pollutions of their nature, hearts and lives; so as, examining themselves thereby, they may come to further conviction of, humiliation for, and hatred against sin, together with a clearer sight of the need they have of Christ, and the perfection of His obedience...'

Robert Shaw explains that the moral law 'being founded in the relations of men to their Creator, and to one another, it retains its authority under all dispensations. In opposition to the Antinomians, who say that believers are released from the obligation of the moral law, our Confession teaches that this law is perpetually binding on justified persons, as well as others. Believers are, indeed, delivered from this law in its covenant form; but they are still under it as a rule of life... Christ, in the most solemn and explicit manner, declared, that he "came not to destroy the law, but to fulfil it" (Matthew 5.17).'[5]

The moral law is essential to the spiritual and moral life of believers in the following three respects. First, it reveals the love of Christ, who so loved them as to obey its precepts and suffer its penalty, that he might deliver them from it as a covenant of works. Second, it shows them the will of God, and regulates their conduct. Third, it serves as a standard of self-examination, and encourages them to a progressive advancement in holiness.

In his interview, Piper has flatly denied all this and left us without a moral compass for the Christian life, making believers vulnerable to moral failure.

The 1689 Baptist Confession of Faith

Piper is a Reformed Baptist, yet this Confession is in full agreement with the Westminster Confession on the matter of God's law. Dr Samuel Waldron, Professor of Systematic Theology, at Midwest Center for Theological Studies, USA, comments on the Confession, 'that the

Reformation itself was in large part a dispute over the relationship of grace and law in the believer's salvation. The position of the Protestant Reformation was that men were justified by grace alone and faith alone without the works of the law... Antinomian teachers... argued that free justification completely freed one from the slavery of the law and that feeling bound to obey the law was slavery.'[6] A practical effect of antinomianism 'is to convey to the popular mind a lessened sense of the majesty of the law of God and of the seriousness and absolute necessity of law-keeping... If anyone speaks to such people of duty and obligation, their response is that such exhortations are legalistic.'[7]

Waldron continues, 'The Confession asserts the fundamental truth that the obligation to obey the law is an inherent and unavoidable part of all human existence... It teaches that the moral law, the Ten Commandments, binds believers.'[8] Waldron explains, 'The Confession carefully qualifies the binding obligation of the law by carefully stating that true believers are not under the law as a covenant of works, but as a rule of life... The final comment of the Confession on the inherent obligation of the law of God is that the law and the gospel do not conflict... The very purpose of the gospel is to deliver men from lawlessness and cause them to obey the law of God (Jeremiah 31.33; Romans 8.4; Titus 2.14).'[9]

Practical consequences

There are so-called 'theoretical antinomians' who, while striving to lead a moral life, insist that the Ten Commandments, as such, are not binding on the believer as the rule of life. A more overt form of antinomianism leads to the unbiblical practice of living without regard to the holiness of God, believing that, since we are saved by faith alone, commandment-keeping is an unnecessary legalistic burden and certainly not essential to the Christian life.

At root all antinomians make the error of emphasising justification at the expense sanctification. While we are justified by faith alone, in Christ alone, apart from works, all believers grow in faith and holiness by keeping God's holy commands—not to gain God's favour, but out of loving obedience to God's Word and a deep gratitude for the grace already bestowed on them through the work of Jesus Christ, their Saviour and Lord. A justification which does not produce the fruit of good works and a striving for personal holiness in a believer's life is no justification at all.

We learn much about Piper's antinomianism from his writings and preaching. He openly downplays the importance of obeying the commandments of God. And as we shall see, he insists that law-keeping is not essential to the Christian life.

An examination of the index of *Desiring God* reveals the extent of Piper's antinomianism. There is only one reference to 'Holiness of God', while 'Happiness of God' is discussed at length in a twenty-page chapter. 'Law of God' and 'Righteousness of God' earn one reference each, 'Obedience' 2, while 'Joy' merits 27, 'Love' 22, and 'Pursuit of Pleasure' and 'Pleasure' together earn 10 references.

We should not be surprised, therefore, that at the heart of Christian Hedonism is a profound antinomianism, which has the following characteristics that become plain as we evaluate Piper's teaching— a neglect of the holiness of God; a disregard for obedience to God's holy law; an indifference to the fear of God; an irreverent style of worship; a superficial view of duty; and a low view of Scripture. These form a connecting chain, each naturally reinforcing the other. An antinomian approach means that a vital dimension of the Christian life is missing— reflection on the holy character of God as revealed in His soul-searching moral law.

Here we should note the strange inconsistency in Piper's teaching. While he insists that Christians must obey *his* 'delight commandment', he does not believe that Christians are under *God's* Ten Commandments.

Passion Conference 2017

In his talk to Passion 2017 entitled, 'The Ultimate Essence of Evil', Piper openly reveals his opposition to law-keeping. He first outlines what he understands to be the ultimate essence of evil. He says that losing a taste for God, or preferring anything or anybody more than God, is the ultimate essence of evil. To quote Piper's words: 'the ultimate essence of evil is the failure to be satisfied in God', and 'The ultimate essence of evil is a preference for other things, other people, anything created more than God, that's the ultimate essence of evil, biblically.' To make it absolutely clear that he does not regard disobedience to God's moral law as important, he boldly declares: 'Disobedience or law-breaking is *not* the ultimate essence of evil.' He also downplays the evil of rebellion, making it a lesser evil than losing 'a taste for God'. This is in sharp contrast to the Psalmist, who declares in a rapture of joy: 'O how love I thy law!' (Psalm 119.97).

Piper's unorthodox view of sin and rebellion comes from his antinomian view of Scripture. According to the Bible, sin is transgression of the law of God and rebellion against God: 'Whosoever committeth sin transgresseth also the law: for sin is the transgression of the law' (1 John 3.4). *Vine's Expository Dictionary* comments on this verse: 'This definition of sin sets forth its essential character as the rejection of the law, or will, of God and the substitution of the will of self.'[10]

And sin is rebellion against God's Word. 'Remember, and forget not, how thou provokedst the LORD thy God to wrath in the wilderness: from the day that thou didst depart out of the land of Egypt, until ye came unto this place, ye have been rebellious against the LORD' (Deuteronomy 9.7). The prophet Samuel told King Saul: 'For rebellion is as the sin of witchcraft, and stubbornness is as iniquity and idolatry. Because thou hast rejected the word of the LORD, he hath also rejected thee from being king' (1 Samuel 15.23).

The Fall of Man

At Passion 2017 Piper goes on to explain to his large audience the ultimate essence of the first, original, world-infecting sin. He reads Genesis 3.1-6, and then quotes Romans 5.12 and says: 'Sin came into the world through one man, and death through sin, and so death spread to billions and billions and billions of people over the thousands of years of human history. You came into the world totally captive to this sin. What's the essence of it? What's the ultimate essence of the first, original, world-infecting sin?' Piper attempts to explain what is happening in the human heart that gives rise to an act of sin. He says that when Eve saw that the forbidden fruit was good food, a delight to the eyes and desirable to make one wise, she reasoned that God wanted to keep it from her. So she took and ate and gave it to her husband. 'We will not be denied what we desire more than God.' Piper asks, 'What was the essence of the Fall of humanity? Was it the eating of the forbidden fruit? No!' He says: 'The moral outrage, the horror of what happened here was that Adam and Eve *desired, desired, desired* this fruit more than God, that's the essence of evil… eating was not the essence of evil, because before they ate they had lost their taste for God, and that's the ultimate outrage in the universe' (Piper's emphasis). Piper adamantly rejects the idea that rebellion against God's authority is more primal than desiring something above God. He openly declares: 'Disobedience to the command of God is not more basic, not more fundamental than what they desired above God.'

But Piper has failed to put his interpretation of the Fall into a proper biblical context, for he did not remind his audience of God's first commandment to Adam. 'And the LORD God commanded the man, saying, Of every tree of the garden thou mayest freely eat: But of the tree of the knowledge of good and evil, thou shalt not eat of it: for in the day that thou eatest thereof thou shalt surely die' (Genesis 2.16-17). According to Scripture, Adam is *commanded* by his Creator not to eat of the tree of the knowledge of good and evil. But in an act of wilful disobedience, Adam and Eve *rebelled* against the *command* of God. (We know, of course, that sin begins in the thought life, but it is rebellion and disobedience even at this stage.)

Piper raises the question: 'Isn't rebellion against God's authority deeper and more primal a problem than the preference of fruit over God?' He presents this question to his large audience of young people, but, as we noted above, he has not told them of God's commandment to Adam.

Clearly in God's eyes the sin of Adam and Eve was disobedience to His command 'thou shalt not eat of it'. Yet Piper sees things differently; he answers his question about rebellion against God's authority thus: 'I've been taught they disobeyed. Period.' And then from antinomian Piper comes an emphatic No! 'Disobedience to the command of God is not more basic, not more fundamental, not more ultimate than what they desired above God.' But Piper's interpretation of the sin of Adam and Eve is wrong and misleading. The apostle Paul is clear: 'For as by one man's disobedience [Adam] many were made sinners, so by the obedience of one [Christ] shall many be made righteous' (Romans 5.19). Paul does *not* discuss a 'more ultimate' desiring of something more than God; under the inspiration of the Holy Spirit he talks of *commandment-breaking*.

Having misled his young audience about the first sin in the Garden of Eden, Piper offers them this advice: 'As long as you see commandment-keeping as the essence of good, and commandment-breaking as the essence of evil, you will never know why you do what you do.' It's not difficult to see that the essence of Piper's teaching is antinomianism. He does not teach that disobedience to God's commandment was mankind's first, original sin against God's holy, righteous character.

We need to emphasise that Piper's teaching is in direct opposition to the teaching of the Westminster Confession (section 1) discussed above. 'God gave to Adam a law, as a covenant of works, by which he bound him, and all his posterity, *to personal, entire, exact, and perpetual obedience*; promising life upon the fulfilling, and threatening death upon the breach of it; and endued him with power and ability to keep it' (my emphasis). Piper's position is so inconsistent that he rejects the Westminster Confession on God's moral law, while using the Westminster Shorter Catechism to support his novel view on the 'chief end of man' (see chapter 6).

Piper's false dichotomy

To emphasise his message that commandment-keeping is not the important thing, Piper goes on to present his audience with a choice between two alternatives. He says with emphasis, 'Obedience to God's commandments, delight in God's character, have you got those two? Which of these is more essential?' Piper is trying to force his audience to choose between obedience to God's commandments and delight in God's character—to make one more essential, and so the other less essential. His aim is to convince his young listeners that 'delight in God' stands above 'obedience to God's commandments'. But Piper has created a false dichotomy, for the two options are not mutually exclusive, but intimately related. Therefore to be asked to choose between them is illegitimate. Christians who delight in God's character are also those who seek to obey His commandments, which reveal God's loving, holy, righteous character. The Ten Commandments, which are a declaration of God's moral law, are for all people for all time. Believers, who love God and delight in His character, also delight in His commandments (Romans 7.22), which are holy, just and good (Romans 7.12), and they, knowing them to be a perfect expression of His perfect character, seek to obey them. Piper's false dichotomy is disingenuous, for it is forcing believers to choose between two essential truths. Such a thing is both theologically wrong and pastorally dangerous —it misleads God's people, especially the young.

It is worth making the point that God's moral law is based on the grace and kindness of God. The Ten Commandments, when obeyed, regulate society for the good of all, as they act as a curb on sin and crime. In addition, God's law convicts of sin, and points the sinner to his need of a Saviour.

Pleasure and duty

In *The Dangerous Duty of Delight*, Piper writes: 'Maximizing our joy in God is what we were created for'.[11] Endorsing the assertion of C.S. Lewis that it is a Christian duty for everyone to be as happy as they can, Piper elaborates: 'Maximum happiness, both qualitatively and quantitatively, is precisely what we are duty-bound to pursue.'[12] He extols the overwhelming importance of Christian Hedonism as a way of life: 'Christian Hedonism is not a game. It is what the whole universe is about. The radical implication is that pursuing pleasure in God is our highest calling.'[13] He says Christ 'is magnified as a glorious treasure when He becomes our unrivalled pleasure… If Christ's honor is our passion, the pursuit of pleasure in Him is our duty.'[14]

Piper explains how Christian hedonists deal with the issue of 'duty'. 'People are often troubled by the teaching of Christian Hedonism that emotions are part of our duty—that they are commanded… But Christian Hedonism says, "Consider the Scriptures." Emotions are commanded throughout the Bible… Therefore Christian Hedonism is not making too much of emotions when it says that being satisfied in God is our calling and duty.'[15] The goal of Christian Hedonism is 'the reunion of pleasure and duty'.[16]

According to Piper, the highest duty of man is to pursue our pleasure in God. In seeking to persuade believers to become Christian hedonists, he writes: 'We will tell them that delight in God is their highest duty.'[17] Explaining Christian Hedonism, he writes: 'We will not try to motivate anyone with appeals to mere duty. We will tell them that in God's presence is full and lasting joy (Psalm 16.11) and *our only duty is to come to him, seeking this pleasure*[18] (Piper's emphasis).

In his article, 'The Joyful Duty of Man', he makes the point that 'for some people—most people—the words "duty" and "law" are not happy words. They tend to sound oppressive and burdensome. So it doesn't sound, then, that God is very loving. That he doesn't have our best interest at heart. Maybe he is so interested in his glory that we don't really count except as slaves to work for him. That kind of objection has to be met.'[19]

He appears to be sympathetic to the view that regards the words 'duty' and 'law' as problematic—guided by his antinomian mindset, he seems to be concerned that certain biblical words might cause an offence to some people and he is determined to do something about that.

Piper's assertions are deeply antinomian, for they ignore the clear teaching of Scripture, which declares that the whole duty of man is to fear God and keep His commandments (Ecclesiastes 12.13). Our Lord said that the highest pursuit of man is to love God with all his heart, soul, mind and strength. And how do we show our love for God? By obeying His commandments—'For this is the love of God, that we keep his commandments: and his commandments are not grievous' (1 John 5.3). Our Lord was clear: 'If ye love me, keep my commandments' (John 14.15). There is no more important pursuit, no greater commandment, no more supreme duty. If any man dreams up a higher calling, as Piper has done, then he has denied the truth of Scripture.

The clear teaching of Scripture is that God is glorified when we obey His commandments because we love and reverence Him, longing to live a holy life and worship Him in the beauty of holiness. 'Give unto the LORD the glory due unto his name; worship the LORD in the beauty of holiness' (Psalm 29.2). Our Lord said: 'Herein is my Father glorified, that ye bear much fruit; so shall ye be my disciples' (John 15.8); and Paul added, 'Being filled with the fruits of righteousness, which are by Jesus Christ, unto the glory and praise of God' (Philippians 1.11). Scripture does not teach that God is glorified by a hedonistic approach to life.

Endnotes

1 Nick Needham, *2000 Years of Christ's Power*, volume 4, 2016, Christian Focus, pp17, 18 and 29

2 'The Antinomian Controversy Rides Again', article by Gary R. Jepsen (Pastor of Pilgrim Lutheran Church, Puyallup, Wash.) http://garyjepsen.com/2016/11/10/178/ on Sola Publishing/WordAlone website

3 Desiring God website, Interview with John Piper, 'Are Christians Under the Ten Commandments?' August 7, 2010, http://www.desiringgod.org/interviews/are-christians-under-the-10-commandments

4 Robert Shaw, *An exposition of the Westminster Confession of Faith*, first published 1845, Christian Focus Publications, 1998 edition, p240

5 Ibid, p245

6 *A Modern Exposition of the 1689 Baptist Confession of Faith*, Samuel E. Waldron, EP Books, 2013, pp294-295

7 Ibid, p296

8 Ibid, p295

9 Ibid, pp296-297

10 W. E. Vine, *Vine's Expository Dictionary of Old & New Testament Words*, Thomas Nelson Inc. 1997, p647

11 John Piper, The *Dangerous Duty of Delight*, 2001, Multinomah, p16

12 Ibid, p14

13 Ibid, p21

14 Ibid, p27

15 Ibid, p30

16 Ibid, p31

17 Desiring God website, article by John Piper, 'Christian Hedonism, Forgive the Label, But Don't Miss the Truth', 1995

18 Desiring God website, article by John Piper, 'What Is Christian Hedonism?' August 2006, www.desiringgod.org/interviews/what-is-christian-hedonism

19 Desiring God website, article by John Piper, 'The Joyful Duty of Man', 1989, http://www.desiringgod.org/messages/the-joyful-duty-of-man

Chapter 4

Piper's Flawed Definition of Love

In *Dangerous Duty*, John Piper gives a definition of love that, quote, 'takes God into account and also includes the feelings that should accompany the outward acts of love: *Love is the overflow and expansion of joy in God, which gladly meets the needs of others*'[1] (Piper's italics).

In chapter four of *Desiring God,* entitled, 'Love: the Labor of Christian Hedonism', Piper quotes from C.S. Lewis's *The Four Loves* (1960) to remind his readers that 'disinterested benevolence toward God is evil'. He says: 'If you come to God dutifully offering Him the reward of your fellowship instead of thirsting after the reward of His fellowship, then you exalt yourself above God as His benefactor and belittle Him as a needy beneficiary—and that is evil.'[2]

Piper asserts that we love and worship God because in Him 'there is fullness of joy; at His right hand are pleasures forevermore (Psalm 16.11)'. This he calls 'vertical Christian Hedonism'. 'Between man and God, on the vertical axis of life, the pursuit of pleasure is not just tolerable; it is mandatory: "Delight yourself in the Lord"! (Psalm 37.4).'[3] Referring to the future reward of loving God, he says, 'So in true Christian Hedonism there is an organic relationship between the love Christ commands and the reward He promises'.[4] He also says that we cannot have real love without real gain.[5] Thus, for Piper, we love God because of what is in it for us.

Piper turns to horizontal Christian Hedonism. 'What about the relationship of love with other people? Is disinterested benevolence the ideal among men? Or is the pursuit of pleasure proper and indeed mandatory for every kind of human love that pleases God? Christian Hedonism answers: *The pursuit of pleasure is an essential motive for every good deed. If you abandon the pursuit of full and lasting pleasure, you cannot love people or please God*[6] (Piper's emphasis).

He concedes that biblical passages come to mind that seem to say exactly the opposite of what Christian Hedonism is saying, such as 1 Corinthians 13.5 ('Love does not seek its own.').[7] Referring to Micah 6.8, Piper writes: 'According to the prophet Micah, God has commanded us not simply to be kind, but to love kindness... Does obedience to the command to "love kindness" mean you must disobey the teaching of 1 Corinthians 13.5 that love should not "seek its own" when you show mercy? No. That is not what Paul is thinking... The moral value of an act of love is not ruined when we are motivated to do it by the anticipation of our own joy in it and from it.'[8] He concludes that 1 Corinthians 13.5 'does not stand in the way Christian Hedonism'.[9]

Piper invites his readers to consider the image of love in two chapters in 2 Corinthians. 'In chapter 8, love is the overflow of joy in God that gladly meets the needs of others... In chapter 2, love is what exists between people when they find their joy in each other's joy... So it is not inconsistent to say that love is the overflow of joy in God that gladly meets the needs of others *and* to say that love is finding your joy in the joy of another. If love is the *labor* of Christian Hedonism, which delights to beget its joy in others, then it is also the *leisure* of Christian Hedonism, which delights to behold this joy begotten in others'[10] (Piper's emphasis).

To help his readers, Piper explains that 'ethicists have tended to distinguish two forms of love as agape and eros, or benevolence and complacency. Not only is there no linguistic basis for such a distinction, but conceptually both resolve into one kind of love at the root. God's agape does not "transcend" His eros, but expresses it. God's redeeming, sacrificial love for His sinful people is described by Hosea in the most erotic terms: "How can I give you up, O Ephraim...?"'[11] He says 'we are told in Hebrews 12.2 by what power Jesus endured suffering: "*For the joy that was set before him* [He] endured the cross, despising the shame..." Should we not infer that in the painful work of redeeming love, God is *very* interested in the satisfaction that comes from His efforts and that He *does* demand the pleasure of a great return on His sacrifice?'[12] (Piper's emphasis).

This utterly false assertion is fundamentally important to Piper's Christian Hedonism. He insists that all love, as it is expressed in good deeds, is motivated by the pursuit of pleasure.[13] By this he means that the *only* love of God and the *only* love of man that will please God are both at root erotic, motivated by self-pleasure. He coins a new definition of love, one that combines both agape and eros—'holy, divine eros'.[14]

From the above it is clear that Piper simply rejects the traditional understanding of 'love' as revealed in the New Testament. While he acknowledges agape and eros as Greek words, he denies that they distinguish between two very different concepts of love.

To summarise thus far: traditionally Christians have understood agape love to be *self-giving* love, and eros love to be *self-seeking* love. Piper denies that they really differ—both distil down into self-love, or Christian Hedonism.

Agape and Eros

Theologian Anders Nygren, in his seminal book, *Agape and Eros* (English edition, 1957), describes the distinction between the two quite different ideas of love.[15] Agape is a biblical word used in the New Testament to describe the Christian concept of self-giving love. Eros is an egocentric word prevalent in the ancient Hellenistic world that is not used in the Bible. Eros could be used in a higher philosophical sense, but in practice had been debased to sexual lust, and therefore is strictly avoided in Holy Scripture.

Eros is a yearning desire which is 'aroused by the attractive qualities of its object; and in Eros-love man seeks God in order to satisfy his spiritual hunger by the possession and enjoyment of the divine perfections'.[16] In Hellenistic religion, Eros does not seek God for His own sake, 'but as the *summum bonum* which alone can satisfy man's wants and needs. That is, it seeks God as a means to an end, the satisfaction of itself, so that what it essentially seeks is not God but its own highest good, which it happens to identify with God... Eros is a love that loves to get, a highly refined form of self-interest and self-seeking.'[17]

Agape love leads to a theocentric view of salvation. The full depth of divine agape is revealed in the incarnation of Jesus Christ and in the Cross of Calvary. 'Agape is a love that loves to give, freely, selflessly...

31

it is opposed to all forms of selfishness, however refined they may be'.[18] 'The God of Agape loves simply because it is His nature to love—and the children of God love because they take after their Father and delight to do as He does.'[19]

Throughout the New Testament the Greek word agape, occurring 106 times, is used for the Christian idea of self-giving love. Opposed to agape is eros. This word is not once used in the New Testament, but is common in Greek literature of the period. It is a love that is extended because of the worth or value or merit of the loved one. It is a love that desires to possess the loved one. It is a love that is fundamentally acquisitive, brings the lover pleasure, and seeks for the lover his own highest good.

Vine's Expository Dictionary

In the original New Testament Greek, agape is described as follows by *Vine's Expository Dictionary*:

Agape and *agapao* are used in the New Testament:

(a) to describe the attitude of God toward His Son, '*And I have declared unto them thy name, and will declare it: that the love wherewith thou hast loved me may be in them, and I in them*' (John 17.26), the human race generally, '*For God so loved the world, that he gave his only begotten Son, that whosoever believeth in him should not perish, but have everlasting life*' (John 3.16), and to those who believe on the Lord Jesus Christ, '*He that hath my commandments, and keepeth them, he it is that loveth me: and he that loveth me shall be loved of my Father, and I will love him, and will manifest myself to him*'(John 14.21);

(b) to convey God's will to His children concerning their attitude one toward another, '*A new commandment I give unto you, That ye love one another; as I have loved you, that ye also love one another*' (John 13.34) and toward all men, '*And the Lord make you to increase and abound in love one toward another, and toward all men, even as we do toward you*' (1 Thess 3.12);

(c) to express the essential nature of God, '*He that loveth not knoweth not God; for God is love*' (1 John 4.8).

Love can be known only from the actions it prompts. God's love is seen in the gift of His Son, '*In this was manifested the love of God toward us, because that God sent his only begotten Son into the world, that we might live through him. Herein is love, not that we loved God, but that he loved us, and sent his Son to be the propitiation for our sins*' (1 John 4.9-10). But obviously this in not the love of complacency, or affection, that is, it was not drawn out by any excellency in its objects, *But God commendeth his love toward us, in that, while we were yet sinners, Christ died for us* (Romans 5.8). It was an exercise of the Divine will in deliberate choice, made without assignable cause save that which lies in the nature of God Himself, (Deut. 7.7,8)...

Christian love has God for its primary object, and expresses itself first of all in implicit obedience to His commandments, '*If ye love me, keep my commandments. He that hath my commandments, and keepeth them, he it is that loveth me: and he that loveth me shall be loved of my Father, and I will love him, and will manifest myself to him*' (John 14.15, 21). Self-will, that is, self-pleasing is the negation of love to God.

Christian love, whether exercised toward the brethren, or toward men generally, is not an impulse from the feelings, it does not always run with the natural inclinations, nor does it spend itself only upon those for whom some affinity is discovered. Love seeks the welfare of all (Romans 15.2), and works no ill to any... In respect of the verb *agapao* as used of God, it expresses the deep and constant love and interest of a perfect Being towards entirely unworthy objects, producing and fostering a reverential love in them towards the Giver, and a practical love towards those who are partakers of the same, and a desire to help others to seek the Giver.[20]

Love Within Limits

Lewis Smedes, Reformed theologian and ethicist, in his book, *Love Within Limits* (1978), correctly comments: 'Agapic love moves us to respond to a neighbor's need with no expectation of reward... It is not interested in the odds of getting some self-satisfaction in return for its efforts.'[21] Its unique character is giving 'without demand of any return. All other loves are different from agape in one crucial way: they all arise from a need and a desire for love's reward. This single ingredient unites all human love as variations of the one natural love we have been calling eros.'[22]

In his critique of *Love Within Limits*, Piper writes: 'The thesis of my critique is, negatively, that agapic love as Smedes defines it has never existed and will never exist in God or man; and positively, that all love resolves into eros in such a way that bad eros seeks satisfaction in bad ways and good eros seeks satisfaction in good ways. Smede's repeated insistence that agapic love never expects *any* return and is never interested in its own satisfaction results, I think, from an incomplete analysis of the psychodynamics of the agapic "impulse" and from a neglect or misunderstanding of a dominant biblical motivation'[23] (Piper's emphasis).

Piper continues, 'in fact agape and eros are one. God's agape does not "transcend" his eros, but expresses it'.[24] Also he says, 'Should we not infer that in the painful work of redeeming love God is *very* interested in the satisfaction that comes from His efforts and that He *does* demand... the pleasure of a great return on his sacrifice' (Piper's emphasis). Referring to the parables of the Wicked Tenants (Matthew 21.33-43), and the Rich Fool (Luke 12.13-21), Piper concludes: 'We may infer rightly that God *does* demand a return on His investment, namely that men glorify Him and give Him thanks' (Piper's emphasis). Piper sums up his understanding of love in these words: 'Recall that agapic love expects no reward and is not interested in self-satisfaction in return for its efforts... I do not think that such disinterested love exists, I suggest another paradigm for human love: God does not cause the believer to *transcend* the desires of eros but rather *redirects* those desired to new objects'[25] (Piper's emphasis). With these words, Piper denies the existence of agape love—he denies that agape love expresses the essential nature of the God of Scripture. So Piper's position appears to be that God's love is at root erotic, acquisitive, and seeks first the benefit of God Himself. Such a God is not the God of the Bible. Here we must note Piper's insistence that agapic love has never existed in God or man. Hence all love in Piper's mind and in his Christian Hedonism is erotic love.

In summary: True agape love in God and in the believer is self-giving, self-denying, and above all, self-sacrificing; but Piper asserts that man loves God because of what pleasure, joy, treasure, and future reward is in it for him. He claims that we do good deeds because doing them gives us personal, sensual, felt pleasure. He repeats his assertion that God loves man because of the pleasure it gives Him, a pleasure that God needs. And Piper redefines the concept of love as only and always motivated by the pleasure it gives to the lover, be that God or man. He denies the existence of agape love, and promotes the idea of 'holy, divine eros'. And most disturbing of all, he denies that the essence of the one true God is agape love.

Endnotes

1   *Dangerous Duty*, p44

2   *Desiring God*, p111

3   Ibid, p111

4   Ibid, p138

5   Ibid, p114

6   *Dangerous Duty*, p39

7   *Desiring God*, p112

8   *Dangerous Duty*, pp40-41

9   Ibid, p42

10   *Desiring God*, pp123-124

11   Ibid, footnote, p124

12   Ibid.

13   *Desiring God*, p141

14   Ibid, footnote, p124

15   Anders Nygren, *Agape and Eros*, complete authorised translation by Philip S. Watson, 1957, SPCK, London.

16   *Agape and Eros*, translator's preface, pviii

17   Ibid, pp xii - xiii

18   Ibid, pxiii

19   Ibid, pxiv

20 *Vine's Expository Dictionary*, pp692-693

21 Lewis Smede, *Love Within Limits*, Eerdmans, 1978, p126

22 Cited from John Piper's article, 'A Christian hedonist looks at *Love Within Limits*, in The Reformed Journal, August 1979, pp9-10

23 Ibid.

24 Ibid, p11

25 Ibid, p12

Chapter 5

Piper's Flawed Understanding of Worship

The longest chapter in *Desiring God*, entitled, 'The Feast of Christian Hedonism', deals with worship. In the 34 pages it takes John Piper to describe 'The Feast' he uses the words *feeling* and *emotion* and *affection* (or derivatives) 97 times. He explains: 'As I use them in this book, the words *feeling* and *emotion* and *affection* do not generally carry different meanings.'[1] As we shall see in this chapter, Piper believes that feelings play a central role in the worship of God.

Perhaps then it's not surprising that Piper is critical of traditional worship, which he regards as cold disinterested worship. He claims that what he calls 'the revolt against hedonism has killed the spirit of worship in many churches and many hearts. The widespread notion that high moral acts must be free from self-interest is a great enemy of true worship... When worship is reduced to disinterested duty, it ceases to be worship. For worship is a feast.'[2] He says, 'Truth without emotions produces dead orthodoxy and a church full (or half-full) of artificial admirers... But true worship comes from people who are deeply emotional and who love deep and sound doctrine'.[3] He thus describes God's Truth as needing man's input to bring life. For Piper, true worship must be highly emotional or it is 'disinterested'.

Piper's hedonistic worship

Piper appears to believe that we worship God not because of who He is but primarily because of who we are. In *Dangerous Duty* Piper writes: 'For worship is the most hedonistic affair of life and must not be ruined with the least thought of disinterestedness. The great hindrance to worship is not that we are a pleasure-seeking people, but that we are willing to settle for such pitiful pleasures.'[4] Piper asserts that 'the hedonistic approach to God in worship is the only humble approach because it is the only one that comes with empty hands. Christian Hedonism pays God the respect of acknowledging (and really feeling!) that He alone can satisfy the heart's longing to be happy. Worship is an end in itself because we glorify God by enjoying Him forever.'[5]

Piper says that 'to honor God in worship, we must not seek Him disinterestedly for fear of gaining some joy in worship and so ruining the moral value of the act. Instead we must seek Him hedonistically, the way a thirsty deer seeks the stream—precisely for the joy of seeing and knowing Him! Worship is nothing less than obedience to the *command* of God: "Delight yourself in the Lord"'[6] (my emphasis). But as we have already seen in chapter 2, Piper's 'delight commandment' is not part of God's law written on tables of stone, but a pastoral exhortation from Psalm 37 to encourage believers in times of adversity. He is using a false commandment to promote a false understanding of worship.

Emotion in worship

Piper continually emphasises what he regards as the vital role of emotion in worship. 'The engagement of the heart in worship is the coming alive of the feelings and emotions and affections of the heart. *Where feelings for God are dead, worship is dead.* True worship must include inward feelings that reflect the worth of God's glory'[7] (Piper's emphasis). He insists that 'Christians are commanded to have God-honoring feelings. We are commanded to feel joy (Philippians 4.4), hope (Psalm 42.5), fear (Luke 12.5), peace (Colossians 3.15), zeal (Romans 12.11), grief (Romans 12.15), desire (1 Peter 2.2), tenderheartedness (Ephesians 4.32), and brokenness and contrition (James 4.9).'[8]

A central plank of Piper's hedonism is his assertion that Christians are 'commanded to experience dozens of emotions, not just to perform acts of willpower'.[9] But common sense and human experience tells us that our emotions are not under the control of human will power. Most emotions are related to external events. They occur spontaneously as a consequence of things that happen in our life. Most emotions are of a temporary fleeting nature. When bad things happen, like failing an important examination, we experience unpleasant emotions like sadness and despondency. When good things happen, like passing an important examination, we feel happy. Our thought life, that is, what we think of and dwell on in our minds, can produce pleasant or unpleasant emotions. The Bible provides many examples of the way sin has a powerful effect on emotions: in the Garden of Eden Adam and Eve felt fear, guilt and shame; King David, after his adultery with Bathsheba, felt sorrow and guilt; the apostle Peter, having publicly denied his Lord three times, wept with shame and remorse. Christians are exhorted to think and meditate on things that are true, honest, just, pure, lovely and of good report (Philippians 4.8). Piper is completely wrong to say that God commands us to produce certain emotions, like joy and happiness, in order to worship Him. Scripture teaches us that Christian joy is far more than an emotion, as discussed in chapter 8. The attempt to produce the fruit of the Spirit by human will power is a futile endeavour. At best, Piper is commanding sentimentality, emotion produced for its own sake.

Piper argues that although all genuine emotion is an end in itself, and is not consciously caused as a means to something else, we can and should seek to have certain feelings. 'We can put ourselves in situations where the feeling may more readily be kindled. We may indeed prize some of the results of these feelings as well as the feelings themselves. But in the moment of authentic emotion, the calculation vanishes. We are transported (perhaps only for seconds) above the reasoning work of the mind, and we experience feeling without reference to logical or practical implications. This is what keeps worship from being "in vain". Worship is authentic when affections for God arise in the heart as an end in themselves.'[10]

Here Piper is trying to convince his readers that the climax of true, authentic worship is an ecstatic emotional feeling, which may last for only seconds, when the worshipper is transported into a mystical place that stands above the working of the rational mind. In this final stage of worship, 'we feel an unencumbered joy in the manifold perfection of God—the joy of gratitude, wonder, hope, admiration.' He quotes Psalm 63.5 and writes: 'In this stage we are satisfied with the excellency of God, and we overflow with the joy of His fellowship. This is the feast of Christian Hedonism.'[11] But Piper's ecstatic and emotionally-centred view of Christian worship is without biblical support and deeply heretical.

Dr Peter Masters, long-standing Pastor of the Metropolitan Tabernacle in London, in *Worship in the Melting Pot* (2002), comments on the danger of ecstatic emotional feeling in worship: '*Ecstatic* worship… aims at stirring the emotions to produce a simulated, emotional state. Ecstatic worship takes place when the object of the exercise is to achieve a warm, happy feeling, perhaps great excitement, and even a sense of God's presence *through the earthly, physical aspects of worship* such as music and movement.' He explains that contrary to this, it should be 'With our minds we appreciate the Lord, His mighty acts, and the doctrines of His Word… it is the mind that must be active and edified. Emotions must be activated by what is recognised in the mind, and not by the direct power of music, rhythms or bodily movement… The new worship, however, is all about music and song being intentionally and blatantly used to have a direct and major influence upon the feelings'[12] (author's own emphasis).

Piper says that worship cannot be done by mere acts of duty. 'It can be done only when spontaneous affections arise in the heart. And these affections for God are an end in themselves. They are the essence of eternal worship.'[13] But this is not true. There are times when believers cannot get the emotions to respond; they worship through the mind alone in an act of loving duty.

He provides this definition: 'Worship is a way of reflecting back to God the radiance of His worth. Now we see that the mirror that catches the rays of His radiance and reflects them back in worship is the joyful heart. Another way of saying this is to say *The chief end of man is to glorify God* by *enjoying Him forever*'[14] (Piper's emphasis).

By his frequent attendance of Passion Conferences we learn much about Piper's approach to worship, for we see with our own eyes the style of worship that he enjoys and endorses. Most of Passion worship is performed in a darkened auditorium that is strafed with flashing strobe lights and filled with thunderous beat music. The response of the audience is to sway to the beat with rhythmic, sensual body movements and wild revelry. At Passion 2017, he was fulsome in his praise of Passion's worldly style of worship. He said:

'One of the things I love about Passion is that Passion celebrates a majestic, holy, glorious, just, beautiful God, and His Son by the Spirit. And then it works its way out in the lyrics of the songs, and various projects to the world that is blind.' Worship leaders at Passion 2017 included Hillsong United, and Christian rap artists Tripp Lee and Lecrae, among others.

Piper ends his chapter on worship with this exhortation: 'Don't let your worship decline to the performance of mere duty. Don't let the childlike awe and wonder be choked out by unbiblical views of virtue. Don't let the scenery and poetry and music of your relationship with God shrivel up and die. You have capacities for joy that you can scarcely imagine. They were made for the enjoyment of God.'[15] This exhortation is designed to lead people into a false, mystical view of worship.

Note how Piper refers to 'unbiblical views of virtue' without explaining what he means. Scripture encourages believers, 'if there be any virtue, and if there be any praise, think on these things' (Philippians 4.8). Note also his disparaging view of 'mere duty'. Yet Scripture is clear that worship is a duty of all true believers. In his sermon expounding Hebrews 10.25, entitled, 'The Duty of Divine Worship', Joseph Watson, an 18th-century Doctor of Divinity, says that 'public worship is the *duty* for all Christians... if we consider what the Church simply is, we can have no other conception of it but of a number of people called together and chosen out of the unbelieving world, to profess the faith of Christ and to worship God according to the instructions which Christ gave.'[16]

John Gill's *Exposition of the Bible* (Gill was a famous 18th-century English Reformed Baptist pastor), interprets the same verse in Hebrews — 'Not forsaking the assembling of ourselves together, as the manner of some is; but exhorting one another: and so much the more, as ye see the day approaching' — thus: 'It is the *duty* of saints to assemble together for public worship, on the account of God, who has appointed it, who approves of it, and whose glory is concerned in it; and on the account of the saints themselves, that they may be delighted, refreshed, comforted, instructed, edified, and perfected; and on account of others, that they may be convinced, converted, and brought to the knowledge and faith of Christ; and in imitation of the primitive saints.'[17]

Comments of Pastor Craig W. Booth

An article entitled, 'A Biblical Study of the Theological Foundation of "Christian Hedonism"', by American Pastor Craig Booth, provides a useful insight into Piper's view of worship. Booth's comments are significant, for he has made a detailed study of Christian Hedonism and written numerous articles on the subject, which can be viewed online at http://thefaithfulword.org/studyhedonism.html.

Booth writes: 'Of all Piper's biblical errors, this one is perhaps the one that causes me the most outrage on behalf of the scriptures and on behalf of genuine believers who are passionately obedient in attempting to follow God's word. Piper makes it quite clear he does not understand the biblical definition of worship, in spite of holding an office as a pastor.'

Booth continues: 'In his book, *Dangerous Duty*, Piper condemns and ridicules the way in which God's bondservants worship, judging them guilty of not participating in "authentic worship" because they do not follow Piper's philosophy of hedonism. This is not merely sad, it is arrogant and outrageous, and I will never understand why the church does not decry such offenses against the Word of God and such wicked accusations by Piper against the people of God.'

Booth goes on: 'Clearly, Piper's writings do not agree with Paul's inspired writings on what worship means, nor is there agreement concerning what it means to have a human body that is living to perform services (labors) of worship. Since a conflict has arisen between Piper's definition of worship (as being an end-state of emotion of the heart devoid of action or service) and Paul's definition of worship (actively using our bodies to teach, serve, edify others) then we must conclude that Piper is wrong and his teaching on worship is, by definition, heresy.'

Booth again: 'According to Piper, worship is exclusively "feelings and emotions and affections of the heart". And he says that "all genuine emotion is an end in itself." Therefore, worship only occurs when "we are transported (perhaps only for seconds) above the reasoning work of the mind and we experience feeling without reference to logical or practical implications." In short, worship is just a feeling.'[18]

Conclusion

The clear implication of Piper's flawed view of worship is that only those who follow *his* doctrine of Christian Hedonism can truly worship God. The truth of the matter is that Christian Hedonism is not worshipping the God of Scripture, but the hedonistic 'God' of Piper's imagination.

Endnotes

1   *Desiring God*, p85 footnote
2   Ibid, p98
3   Ibid, pp81-82
4   *Dangerous Duty*, p55
5   *Desiring God*, pp95-96
6   Ibid, p98
7   Ibid, pp87-88
8   Ibid, p89
9   Ibid, p300
10 Ibid, p92
11 Ibid, p96
12 Peter Masters, *Worship in the Melting Pot*, Wakeman Trust, London,2002, pp23 and26, also at https://www.the-highway.com/worship3_Masters.html
13 *Desiring God*, p92
14 Ibid, p94
15 Ibid, p108
16 Joseph Watson, sermon, 'The Duty of Divine Worship', http://biblehub.com/sermons/auth/watson/the_duty_of_divine_worship.htm
17 John Gill's *Exposition of the Bible* commentary, http://www.biblestudy-tools.com/commentaries/gills-exposition-of-the-bible/hebrews-10-25.html
18 Craig W. Booth, A Biblical Study of the Theological Foundation of "Christian Hedonism", 2002, http://www.thefaithfulword.org/studyhedonism.html

Chapter 6

Piper's Happy God

In his twenty-page chapter on 'The Happiness of God' in *Desiring God*, John Piper sets out to show us the ultimate ground for Christian Hedonism. He writes: 'The bedrock foundation of Christian Hedonism is not God's allegiance to us, but to Himself. If God were not infinitely devoted to the preservation, display, and enjoyment of His own glory, we could have no hope of finding happiness in Him.'[1] He quotes Psalm 115.3, 'Our God is in the heavens; he does all that he pleases.' He offers this interpretation: 'God has the right and power to do whatever makes Him happy. That is what it means to say that God is sovereign... And if none of His purposes can be frustrated, then He must be the happiest of all beings. This infinite, divine happiness is the fountain from which the Christian Hedonist drinks and longs to drink more deeply.'[2] Piper confidently declares, 'the foundation of Christian Hedonism is the happiness of God'.[3] So the God at the root of Christian Hedonism is a happy God who is free to do whatever pleases Him, whatever He enjoys most, whatever gives Him most happiness. This is pure hedonism.

Piper's happy God

Though none of the serious English translations of Scripture refer to God as 'happy', still Piper is determined to promote his concept of the 'happy God'. He does this with inventive interpretations of Scripture. In *The Pleasures of God* (1991), he asks us to consider what he calls 'a beautiful phrase in 1 Timothy 1.11 buried beneath the too-familiar surface of Bible buzzwords. Before we dig it up, it sounds like this: "The gospel of the glory of the blessed God." But after you dig it up, it sounds like this: "The good news of the glory of the happy God".'[4] So with a clever 'digging up' of Scripture (others might call it a clever manipulation of Scripture) Piper is able to change the 'blessed God' of Scripture into the 'happy God' of Christian Hedonism.

In seeking to justify his phrase the 'happy God', Piper admits that most versions of Scripture translate the original Greek in 1 Timothy 1.11 like this: 'the *glorious* gospel of the blessed God'. But he then refers to 2 Corinthians 4.4 where what he terms a 'similar phrase' is often translated as 'the gospel of the *glory of Christ*' (Piper's emphasis). He argues that the same principle of translation should be used in 1 Timothy 1.11, which he would then translate as, 'The good news of the glory of the happy God'.[5] He says the word translated 'blessed' in both of these verses (*makarios*) is the same one used in the Beatitudes, and it means 'happy' or 'fortunate'. Piper writes: 'Paul himself uses it in other places to refer to the happiness of the person whose sins are forgiven (Romans 4.7); or the person whose conscience is clear (Romans 14.22).'[6] Again Piper is misleading his readers. The ESV and NIV translations use the word 'blessed' in both these verses; the KJV translates Romans 4.7 as 'blessed', and Romans 14.22 as 'happy is he that condemneth not himself' (both the NKJV and the NASB follow suit). Here we see how he is suggesting that in Scripture the words 'happy' and 'blessed' have the identical meaning and therefore there is no distinction between them.

But Piper does not tell his readers that in the ESV the word 'blessed' occurs 291 times and the word 'happy' only 8 times, and then not once in the New Testament. Every occurrence of 'happy' in Scripture refers to human beings who are experiencing a pleasant emotion in favourable circumstances. 'Happy' is never used in Scripture in reference to God. And Piper makes no attempt to explain the difference in meaning of 'blessed' and 'happy'. On the basis of his convoluted reasoning, he concludes: 'So 1 Timothy is referring to the gospel of the *happy* God'[7] (Piper's emphasis).

But we cannot accept Piper's 'digging up' of Scripture. Notice his pejorative reference to 'Bible buzzwords' and his need to 'dig up' the Bible to make it say that which suits his agenda. By his subtle reinterpretation he has made Scripture appear to support his concept of a 'happy God'. But the plain reading of Scripture refers to the blessed God, who is holy, righteous and good. Piper asserts that, quote, 'a great part of God's glory is His happiness. It was inconceivable to the apostle Paul that God could be denied infinite joy and still be all glorious. To be infinitely glorious was to be infinitely happy. He uses the phrase, "the glory of the happy God", because it is a glorious thing for God to be as happy as he is. God's glory consists much in the fact that he is happy beyond our wildest imagination. And this is the gospel: "The gospel of the glory of the happy God". It is good news that God is gloriously happy. No one would want to spend eternity with an unhappy God.'[8]

But this is completely wrong, for the apostle Paul never refers to God as the 'happy God'. In his first letter to Timothy, Paul used the Greek word *makarios* twice. In 1 Timothy 1.11, as we saw above, he writes: 'According to the glorious gospel of the *blessed* God, which was committed to my trust', and in 1 Timothy 6.15, he refers to God as 'the *blessed* and only Potentate, the King of kings, and Lord of lords'. These are the only two occasions when *makarios* is used of God in the whole New Testament. The other uses of *makarios* (particularly in the Beatitudes) describe the blessed state of human beings, usually in the context of obeying or emulating God. *Vine's Expository Dictionary*, commenting on this usage, says: 'In the beatitudes the Lord indicates not only the characters that are blessed, but the nature of that which is the highest good.'[9] In other words, with the *makarios* word mere 'happiness' is not in view, but a far more exalted state, seen supremely in God Himself and reflected in His believing people. So to allege that Paul believed God is best understood to be a 'happy God' is plain wrong and a gross theological error.

In his letter to the Ephesians Paul uses the Greek word *eulogetos*, which, according to *Vine's Expository Dictionary*, 'means blessed, praised; it applies only to God'.[10] He writes: 'Blessed be the God and Father of our Lord Jesus Christ who has blessed us with all spiritual blessings in heavenly places in Christ' (Ephesians 1.3). In 2 Corinthians he again uses *eulogetos* when he writes: 'Blessed be God, even the Father of our Lord Jesus Christ, the Father of mercies, and the God of all comfort' (2 Corinthians 1.3).

Piper makes the point that the happiness of God is a foundational doctrine of Christian Hedonism. He writes: 'Therefore if God is not a happy God, Christian Hedonism has no foundation. For the aim of the Christian Hedonist is to be happy in God, to delight in God, to cherish and enjoy His fellowship and favor… Therefore the foundation of Christian Hedonism is the happiness of God.'[11] We must conclude, however, that Piper's Christian Hedonism is purely of his own invention and has no legitimate basis in the divinely inspired Word of God.

Happy or blessed?

Piper attempts to use Scripture to justify his concept of the 'happy God'. But the God of Scripture is not the happy God of Christian Hedonism, but the 'blessed' God and Father of our Lord Jesus Christ. Here it is important to understand the difference between happy and blessed. Dr George Wood of the Assemblies of God, in his article, 'Happy or Blessed?', gives a clear exposition of the difference: 'Happy, or happiness, comes from the Old English word hap. Hap, happy, happiness are all related to the word happened. Happiness is a happening. It is a spirit of joy or exhilaration produced by an outside event. Happiness is a product of circumstance. It results from an external cause. By its very nature, it cannot be enduring because life's circumstances do not continually produce happy moments. Jesus' promise of blessing, however, embraces you in both good and bad circumstances, so we must press further to get the meaning of this word... However, when we turn to the pages of the New Testament, the words blessed and blessing (which occur seventy-two and eighteen times in the NIV, respectively) are never used to refer to external prosperity. Always it refers to an inward condition.'[12]

So we see that happiness is pretty much a humanistic, secular concept, while being blessed refers to divine favour. Happiness is what the world is seeking after in its fallen and sinful state, but blessedness comes from doing what is right and obeying God's Word. 'Blessed is the man that walketh not in the counsel of the ungodly, nor standeth in the way of sinners, nor sitteth in the seat of the scornful. But his delight is in the law of the LORD; and in his law doth he meditate day and night' (Psalm 1.1-2). And, 'Blessed are the undefiled in the way, who walk in the law of the LORD. Blessed are they that keep his testimonies, and that seek him with the whole heart' (Psalm 119.1-2). These verses remind us that, contrary to Piper's antinomianism, blessedness is to be found in joyful law-keeping. So while happiness is something circumstances do for us, being blessed is something God does for us. The man blessed by

God can experience the joy of the Lord even though the circumstances are not good.

Puritan theology understood the meaning of the blessedness of God. Puritan sympathiser Lewis Bayly in his once massively influential devotional handbook, *The Practice of Piety, directing a Christian how to walk that he may please God* (date of third edition 1613), enumerated the divine attributes and then added, 'From all these attributes ariseth one, which is God's sovereign blessedness or perfection.' He went on to define blessedness as 'that perfect and immeasurable possession of joy and glory, which God hath in himself for ever, and is the cause of all the bliss and perfection that every creature enjoys in its measure'.[13] In sharp contrast to Puritan theology based on Scripture, stands Piper's trivial concept of the 'happy God', based on the philosophy of Christian Hedonism.

The chief end of God

In *Desiring God,* Piper asserts that 'The ultimate ground of Christian Hedonism is the fact that God is uppermost in His own affections: *The chief end of God is to glorify God and enjoy Himself forever*' (Piper's emphasis). He argues that the redemption and salvation of sinners are not God's ultimate goal; he says God performs these acts 'for the sake of something greater: namely, the enjoyment He has in glorifying Himself'.[14] He has reworked the concept of God's glory to mean, 'the *enjoyment* He has in glorifying Himself' (my emphasis). This statement is misleading. We agree that the manifestation of God's glory in Christ is God's great goal in Creation, the Fall and Redemption (Ephesians 1. 6,12,14), but not in the way Piper expresses it. He has cleverly mixed truth and error.

Piper paints the picture of a God whose chief attribute is happiness and whose chief end is to enjoy Himself. In other words, Piper's God is a committed hedonist. This is a false view of the God of the Bible. While Scripture says nothing about the 'chief end of God', it says much about the holiness, justice and righteousness of God. But Piper, seeking to support his hedonistic cause, claims to know the chief end of the eternal, infinite God, whose ways and thoughts are beyond human understanding. Scripture says, 'no man can find out the work that God maketh from the beginning to the end' (Ecclesiastes 3.11). And, 'For what man knoweth the things of a man, save the spirit of man which is in him? even so the things of God knoweth no man, but the Spirit of God' (1 Corinthians 2.11). 'For my thoughts are not your thoughts, neither are your ways my ways, saith the LORD. For as the heavens are higher than the earth, so are my ways higher than your ways, and my thoughts than your thoughts.' (Isaiah 55.8-9). Many things known to God are kept secret from man. 'The secret things belong unto the LORD our God: but those things which are revealed belong unto us and to our children for ever, that we may do all the words of this law' (Deuteronomy 29.29). The things which are revealed by God in His Word and in Creation are the proper object of our enquiries, that we may know our duty and be kept from useless speculation about the secret things of God, such as the 'chief end of God', which is *not* revealed to mankind, except in so far as God's glory in Christ is to be manifested. Piper's statement that the chief end of God is to *enjoy Himself forever* is seriously misleading.

Preserving God's diminishing glory

In responding to the question, 'What is it about redemptive history that delights the heart of God'? Piper writes: 'My conclusion is that God's own glory is uppermost in his own affections. In everything He does *His purpose is to preserve* and display that glory. To say that His own glory is uppermost in His own affections means that He puts a greater value on it than on anything else. He delights in His glory above all things'[15] (my emphasis).

Piper goes on, 'God's ultimate goal is to *preserve* and display His infinite and awesome greatness and worth, that is, His glory'[16] (my emphasis). God seeks to display His glory for 'He loves His glory infinitely'.[17] God's glory 'is clearly the uppermost reality in His affections. He loves Himself infinitely'.[18] And more, 'This is why God has done all things from creation to consummation *for the preservation* and display of His glory. All His works are simply the spillover of His infinite exuberance for His own excellence'[19] (my emphasis).

Piper tells us that God needs to *preserve* His glory, as if it were subject to spoilage and decay like some food stuff. He claims that 'God has done all things, from creation to consummation, for the *preservation* and display of His glory' (my emphasis). The clear inference is that God's glory is unstable and therefore needs to be preserved.

But the glory of God, which is a manifestation of all His attributes together, is eternal and will never pass away. So the glorious God of the Bible does not need to preserve or add to His glory. Human beings do not need to build up God's glory. Glory is an inherent part of God's self-existence; a manifestation of who He is. God's glory is revealed in Creation. 'The heavens declare the glory of God' (Psalm 19.1). His glory is revealed in His Son and in the Cross. The Lord Jesus said, 'Now is the Son of man glorified, and God is glorified in him. If God be glorified in him, God shall also glorify him in himself, and shall straightway glorify him' (John 13.31-32). So the glory of God stands forever, and does not need to be preserved. For Piper to imply that God's glory needs to be preserved is a serious error, but follows naturally from his concept of a hedonistic God.

The chief end of man

Piper hijacks a famous statement from the Westminster Shorter Catechism to support his doctrine of Christian Hedonism. The Shorter Catechism declares: 'Man's chief end is to glorify God, *and* to enjoy him for ever' (my emphasis). Piper has distorted this statement by replacing the 'and' with 'by', so: 'The chief end of man is to glorify God *by* enjoying Him forever.'

Piper's bold rewriting of probably the most famous theological statement ever written suggests that God needs our enjoyment of Him or our satisfaction in Him in order to maintain His glory. God is not just a *hedonist*, He also *needs* our help to keep His glory intact. Piper believes that both God and man need to pursue hedonistic pleasure. Thus he tries to find a divine command to support the search for personal pleasure.

He hopes his cleverly amended Shorter Catechism will convince the reader that the pursuit of joy and pleasure is *commanded* by God. In this attempt, he not only misquotes a godly catechism but also, as we saw in chapter 2, misinterprets a phrase from Psalm 37, and all in the service of bolstering his flimsy edifice of Christian Hedonism.

Dr Nick Needham, in the fourth volume of his Church history, *2000 Years of Christ's Power*, comments on this famous statement from the Shorter Catechism. Explaining the meaning of the word 'enjoy' as used in the Catechism, he writes: '*Enjoy* here has the older sense of "share in", "experience", "receive the benefit of", as the proof-texts indicate.' [20] So the modern sense of enjoying *pleasure* is not meant, but rather receiving the blessings of a life lived in time and eternity for God's glory. Piper is actually proceeding on a false premise when he rewrites this statement.

What is the chief end of man? Scripture tells us that the *whole duty* of man is to fear God and obey His commandments. The apostle Peter instructs believers, who have been redeemed by the precious blood of Christ, who are kept by the power of God and who face fiery trials of faith, 'As obedient children, not fashioning yourselves according to the former lusts in your ignorance: but as he which hath called you is holy, so be ye holy in all manner of conversation; Because it is written, Be ye holy; for I am holy' (1 Peter 1.14-16).

The Preacher in Ecclesiastes (Solomon) shows that human wisdom is limited, for it cannot find out the larger purposes of God. The Preacher also reveals the futility of pleasure-seeking. Ecclesiastes concludes: 'Let us hear the conclusion of the whole matter: Fear God, and keep his commandments: for this is the whole duty of man. For God shall bring every work into judgment, with every secret thing, whether it be good, or whether it be evil' (Ecclesiastes 12.13-14).

Our Lord, in response to the question, 'Which is the first commandment of all?' answered, 'The first of all the commandments is, Hear, O Israel; The Lord our God is one Lord: And thou shalt love the Lord thy God with all thy heart, and with all thy soul, and with all thy mind, and with all thy strength: this is the first commandment. And the second is like, namely this, Thou shalt love thy neighbour as thyself. There is none other commandment greater than these.' (Mark 12.28-31). In His reply the Lord has summarised the Ten Commandments and set them forth as our model of godly living.

In responding to the question regarding the most important commandment of God, the Lord could have referred to the 'chief end of man', if that was something He wanted His people to understand, but He did not do so. Rather our Lord emphasised that the greatest commandment is to love God and the second to love our neighbour. These two are the greatest of all commandments, and we show our love for God by obeying His commandments.

So while Piper speaks about glorifying God by enjoying Him, Scripture teaches us about the most important commandment, and about the whole duty of man. We glorify God by knowing His laws and by obeying them out of a sense of loving duty.

Conclusion

The so-called 'happiness of God' is the central doctrine of Christian Hedonism. Piper writes: 'Therefore if God is not a happy God, Christian Hedonism has no foundation. For the aim of the Christian Hedonist is to be happy in God, to delight in God, to cherish and enjoy His fellowship and favour... Therefore the foundation of Christian Hedonism is the happiness of God.'[21] Piper's 'happy God' is purely of his own invention and has no legitimate basis in the revealed Word of God. We must therefore conclude that Christian Hedonism has no foundation in Scripture.

Endnotes

1   *Desiring God*, p31
2   Ibid, p32
3   Ibid, p33
4   John Piper, *The Pleasures of God*, Multnomah Press, 1991, p23
5   Ibid, p23
6   Ibid, p41
7   Ibid, pp40-41
8   Ibid, p23
9   *Vine's Expository Dictionary*, p125
10   Ibid, p125
11   *Desiring God*, pp32-33
12   George O Wood, 'Happy or Blessed?', http://georgeowood.com/happy-or-blessed/

13   Cited from 'The Gospel of the Glory of the Blessed God', an article by Fred Sanders, January 2015, from website of Alliance of Confessing Evangelical, Reformation 21, http://www.reformation21.org/articles/the-gospel-of-the-glory-of-the-blessed-god.php

14   *Desiring God*, p31

15   Ibid, p42

16   Ibid, p42

17   Ibid, p43

18   Ibid, p43

19   Ibid, p45

20   Nick Needham, *2000 years of Christ's Power*, vol.4 footnote no. 12 on p251

21   *Desiring God*, pp32-33

Chapter 7

Manipulating Scripture

John Piper claims to believe in the inerrancy of Scripture. His own church statement of faith, the Bethlehem Affirmation, affirms: 'We believe that the Bible is the Word of God, fully inspired and without error in the original manuscripts, written under the inspiration of the Holy Spirit, and that it has supreme authority in all matters of faith and conduct.'[1] He explains how he endeavours to ensure that he interprets Scripture accurately: 'I have tried to develop over the years a very intense and rigorous and detailed and attentive habit of reading Scripture closely and carefully, not loosely, flippantly, carelessly, proof-texting my preferences. But really test my thoughts by thinking the thoughts of the biblical writers after them by a rigorous, intense, close, careful, detailed attention to the train of thought that they develop in their writing... And the last thing I would say is I pray constantly that God will lead me into truth and in paths of righteousness and that he will keep my tongue from evil and my lips from speaking deceit.'[2]

He has built up a reputation as a sound biblical expositor, committed to biblical truth. And so it is no surprise that in his book, *Desiring God*, he refers to 650 biblical verses, creating the impression of a book soundly based on Scripture. Psalm 37.4, the verse Piper has used to invent his 'delight commandment', is used ten times in the book. His book, *The Pleasures of God*, has a twelve-page Scripture index of 951 biblical references. This produces an overwhelming impression that Piper is a deeply biblical man.

Despite his assertion that he believes in the inerrancy of Scripture, and his 'detailed and attentive habit of reading Scripture closely and carefully', he frequently quotes Scripture out of context and even removes words from a verse to change its meaning. In other words, Piper's claim to believe in the inerrancy of Scripture is not consistent with the way he uses Scripture. In his discussion of conversion, he observes that 'It does no good to tell these people to believe in the Lord Jesus. *The phrase is empty*'[3] (my emphasis). The biblical phrase 'believe in the Lord Jesus', is labelled by Piper as 'empty'. Every reader should question an author who labels any phrase in God's Word as 'empty'. Our Lord said, 'Till heaven and earth pass, one jot or one tittle shall in no wise pass from the law, till all be fulfilled' (Matthew 5.18).

Piper goes on to explain that he prefers the phrase, 'Do you receive Jesus as your *Treasure*?' (Piper's emphasis). He then asks, 'Could it be that today the most straightforward biblical command for conversion is not, "Believe in the Lord," but, "Delight yourself in the LORD"?'[4] Yet when the Roman jailer appealed to Paul and Barnabas: 'Sirs, what must I do to be saved?' they replied with a concise statement of the way of salvation, 'Believe on the Lord Jesus Christ, and thou shalt be saved, and thy house' (Acts 16.31). But this biblical phrase is not good enough for Piper. Obviously, unfamiliar concepts must be explained in evangelism, but Piper is seeking to insert the ideas of Christian Hedonism, thereby replacing biblical 'repentance toward God, and faith toward our Lord Jesus Christ' (Acts 20.21).

In chapter 6 we saw Piper skilfully manipulate Scripture to make it appear to say that the 'blessed God' is really the 'happy God'. There he asked his readers to consider what he calls 'a beautiful phrase in 1 Timothy 1.11 buried beneath the too-familiar surface of Bible buzzwords. Before we dig it up, it sounds like this: "The gospel of the glory of the blessed God." But after you dig it up, it sounds like this: "The good news of the glory of the happy God".'[5] So by cleverly manipulating Scripture, he was able to change the 'blessed God' of Scripture into the 'happy God' of Christian Hedonism.

Deuteronomy 28.47-48

In *Desiring God*, Piper presents the argument that 'The Word of God *commands* us to pursue our joy' (my emphasis). To support this argument he refers to Deuteronomy 28.47-48, and offers this interpretation: 'the Word of God threatens terrible things if we will not be happy: Because you did not serve the LORD your God with joyfulness and gladness of heart, because of the abundance of all things, therefore you shall serve your enemies whom the LORD will send against you (Deuteronomy 28:47-48)'.[6] These verses are central to much of his 'delighting in God' thesis. Yet, as we shall see, they are taken out of context and woefully misinterpreted.

In *Dangerous Duty*, Piper attempts to show that Christian Hedonism 'is an old-fashioned way of life', not something new. Again, he quotes Deuteronomy 28.47-48, which he redacts and quotes out of context. Piper's exact quote is: 'Because you did not serve the LORD your God with joy and a glad heart... therefore you shall serve your enemies (Deuteronomy 28:47-48)'. He claims that Moses 'threatened terrible things if we would not be happy'.[7]

He seeks to make Scripture say that God will judge Israel for not being joyful and not serving Him with gladness of heart. But in actuality the whole of Deuteronomy chapter 28 is the listing of blessings for obedience (vv1-14) and curses for disobedience (vv15-68) to the laws of God. The main point of chapter 28 is to provide the strongest possible warning of the curse that comes from *disobedience to God's commandments*: 'But it shall come to pass, if thou wilt not hearken unto the voice of the LORD thy God, to observe to do all his commandments and his statutes which I command thee this day; that all these curses shall come upon thee, and overtake thee' (Deuteronomy 28.15). So the reason for God's threatened anger and punishment of Israel is not because Israel might fail to 'serve with joy and a glad heart' (Piper's words), but because they might fail to obey His commandments. Piper has here twisted Scripture to make it appear that God commanded Israel to pursue their joy or suffer terrible things. The simple inclusion of verses 45-46 produces an entirely different picture: 'Moreover all these curses shall come upon thee, and shall pursue thee, and overtake thee, till thou be destroyed; *because thou hearkenedst not unto the voice of the LORD thy God, to keep his commandments and his statutes which he commanded thee*: And they shall be upon thee for a sign and for a wonder, and upon thy seed for ever' (Deuteronomy 28.45-46). Piper attempts to convince his readers that lack of joy and gladness was what brought God's judgment on the nation—not disobedience to God's laws. So he has twisted Scripture to make it appear that God commanded Israel to pursue their joy. If the nation could only produce joy and gladness of heart, all would be well. Disobedience to God's commandments, in Piper's mind, is not important! His antinomianism is again evident.

Verses 47-48 are a proof-text favourite of Piper, often used to establish his thesis of hedonism. We see how he has blatantly ripped two verses of Scripture out of their context and then misinterpreted them in order to lead people into the broad way of Christian Hedonism.

In his address to Passion 1997, Piper referred to Deuteronomy 28.47-48 to support his case for Christian Hedonism. With great emphasis he said to a large audience: 'Is that a warrant for hedonism or what? Is that a warrant for making it your life vocation to pursue your joy in God with all your might?'[8]

In a keynote address given to the prestigious New Canaan Society in America in 2015, entitled, 'It Is Right to Live for Maximum Pleasure: Eight Reasons from the Bible', Piper yet again used Deuteronomy 28.47-48 and made this amazing statement, 'You go to hell if you are not happy in God.'[9] This absurd statement tells us much about John Piper. We see again how he twists Scripture to promote his dogma of hedonism. We see him threatening eternal damnation as a ploy to frighten people into following his Christian Hedonism.

Piper's repeated use of his false interpretation of Deuteronomy 28 raises the question: Why has he not corrected his error? It seems inconceivable he has not been challenged by his peers. One does not need to be a theologian to see the gross error here. Piper first used his erroneous interpretation in *Desiring God* in 1986; he repeated the same error a decade later in his Passion talk 1997, and again in *Dangerous Duty* in 2001, and again in a keynote address to the New Canaan Society in 2015. So over a period of three decades, Piper has continued with the same flawed use of Scripture to promote his ideology of hedonism. His claim to have developed 'over the years a very intense and rigorous and detailed and attentive habit of reading Scripture closely and carefully, not loosely, flippantly, carelessly...' is disingenuous in the extreme, to say the very least. As a committed antinomian, he has avoided the true reason for God's anger, namely Israel's disobedience to God's law. Piper's handling of Deuteronomy 28 is shameful, and totally discredits his dogma of Christian Hedonism, and leaves his reputation as a sound Bible teacher in tatters.

Paul the hedonist

Piper writes into Scripture the idea that the apostle Paul was a Christian Hedonist. In dealing with 2 Corinthians 1.23-2.4, he invites us to notice 'how Paul's pursuit of their joy and his own joy relates to love'. He goes on: 'When *this* joy abounds in his converts, Paul feels great joy himself, and he unashamedly tells them that the reason he does not want to rob them of their joy is that this would rob him of *his* joy. This is the way a Christian Hedonist talks' (Piper's emphasis). Piper concludes that Paul did not want to be pained. 'He wants joy, not pain. He is a Christian Hedonist!'[10]

He goes on to refer to a 'tearful experience' that comes 'when Paul uncovers his commitment to Christian Hedonism. In Acts 20 he gathers for the last time with elders of the church at Ephesus. There are many tears and much embracing as Paul finishes his farewell address (20.37)... The last thing Paul left ringing in their ears on the beach at Miletus was the ministerial charge of Christian Hedonism: "It is more blessed to give than to receive".'[11]

Piper is attempting to make the point that because Paul had joy in Christ he was a hedonist. But this is plain wrong, for all Christians have the joy of Christ in their hearts. Our Lord said: 'These things have I spoken unto you, that my joy might remain in you, and that your joy might be full' (John 15.11). He has misrepresented Scripture in his attempt to make the apostle Paul appear to be a Christian Hedonist. Hedonism has so consumed Piper's thinking that he attempts to force everything and everyone, even the apostle Paul, into its pleasure-seeking mould.

Jesus is a Christian Hedonist

Piper is asked the question: 'Pastor John, is Jesus a Christian Hedonist? If so, what would be your primary proofs from the Bible?'[12]

He replies: 'Yes. Without the slightest hesitation, Jesus lived to glorify His Father by enjoying Him as the sustaining power in all His suffering and by seeking to enjoy Him forever on the other side of the greatest suffering and by means of the greatest suffering. So, that is what I mean by being a Christian Hedonist. And, to boot, He taught us to be motivated in the same way.'

One of Piper's biblical proofs is the High Priestly Prayer in John 17. He says Christ's 'consummated joy with the Father would one day be ours. That is what He was pursuing, and that is what He wants us to pursue.'

He says Jesus 'told us to make this joy in God our top priority. That is what the command to love God with all the heart means... He becomes our supreme treasure. So, when Jesus says, "You shall love the Lord your God with all your heart" (Matthew 22.37), He means: find God to be your heart's total satisfaction. What else could He mean? Find His beauty and His glory, His justice, His goodness, His truth, everything there is about Him, find that to be your heart's treasure. It is what love God with all the heart means.' But Piper is wrong. The Lord Jesus said: 'If ye love me, keep my commandments' (John 14.15), and 'If a man love me, he will keep my words: and my Father will love him, and we will come unto him, and make our abode with him' (John 14.23).

As is his practice, Piper quotes a list of other verses, and interprets them through the lens of his hedonistic thinking (Hebrews 12.2; Matthew 6.19; Matthew 25.21, 23; Mark 10.28; Mark 10.29–30; Luke 12.33; Luke 14.13–14; Acts 20.35) and then concludes: 'So, my answer is yes. Jesus was a Christian Hedonist. He is today a Christian Hedonist, I would argue — that could be another APJ [Ask Pastor John] — the best one ever. Jesus was the best Christian Hedonist who ever existed, both in His own motivation and in His teaching about motivation.'[13]

In his attempt to make the Lord Jesus appear to be a hedonist, Piper entirely ignores our Lord's teaching on self-denial and the need for obedience to God's moral law. The assertion that Jesus is a hedonist must be seen in the context of Piper's ministry. As we saw in chapter 3, he says openly that Christians are no longer under the Ten Commandments: 'No. The Bible says we're not under the law.' He is a practising antinomian who is dismissive of law-keeping. Indeed, his antinomianism is an essential component of his Christian Hedonism. But the Lord Jesus, who obeyed God's law perfectly, was not an antinomian. He said: 'Think not that I am come to destroy the law, or the prophets: I am not come to destroy, but to fulfil. For verily I say unto you, Till heaven and earth pass, one jot or one tittle shall in no wise pass from the law, till all be fulfilled. Whosoever therefore shall break one of these least commandments, and shall teach men so, he shall be called the least in the kingdom of heaven' (Matthew 5.17-19). Pleasure-seeking was not the objective of the Lord's ministry. While Piper teaches that the duty of every believer is to pursue their maximum pleasure 24/7 in God,[14] our Lord taught His disciples to deny themselves and take up their cross, *daily*, and follow Him, not pleasure.

Piper's ridiculous assertion that Jesus Christ is a hedonist has massive implications for Christian theology. The Lord Jesus is the exact representation of His Father. 'I and my Father are one'. If God the Son is a hedonist, then God the Father is a hedonist. Piper is making the eternal God a hedonist, and radically changing our understanding of the nature and character of the one true God.

Piper's deceptive manipulation of Scripture and his heretical labelling of the apostle Paul and our Lord Jesus Christ as hedonists, raises serious questions about his ministry. Our Lord warned about false prophets (today we would say false teachers), and said we would know them by their fruits (Matthew 7.15,20). He also said: 'Not every one that saith unto me, Lord, Lord, shall enter into the kingdom of heaven; but he that doeth the will of my Father which is in heaven. Many will say to me in that day, Lord, Lord, have we not prophesied in thy name? and in thy name have cast out devils? and in thy name done many wonderful works? And then will I profess unto them, I never knew you: depart from me, ye that work iniquity' (Matthew 7.21-23). And so, in view of the evidence presented in this book, we must face the sobering question: Is John Piper a false teacher?

Endnotes

1   Desiring God website, article by John Piper, '2 Birthdays and Biblical Inerrancy', June 18, 2008, http://www.desiringgod.org/articles/2-birthdays-and-biblical-inerrancy

2   Desiring God website, Ask Pastor John interview, 'How Do I Test My Interpretations of the Bible?', September 2016, http://www.desiringgod.org/interviews/how-do-i-test-my-interpretations-of-the-bible

3   *Desiring God*, p55

4   Ibid.

5   *The Pleasures of God*, p23

6   *Desiring God*, pp293-294

7   *Dangerous Duty*, p10

8   Piper Passion 1997, www.desiringgod.org/messages/passion-for-the-supremacy-of-god-part-2

9   Desiring God website, 'It Is Right to Live for Maximum Pleasure: Eight Reasons from the Bible, 1 May, 2015, Piper sermon to the New Canaan Society, http://www.desiringgod.org/messages/it-is-right-to-live-for-maximum-pleasure

10   *Desiring God*, p122

11   Ibid, p125

12   Desiring God website, Ask Pastor John, 'Was Jesus a Christian Hedonist?' http://www.desiringgod.org/interviews/was-jesus-a-christian-hedonist

13   Ibid.

14   Desiring God website, 'It Is Right to Live for Maximum Pleasure: Eight Reasons from the Bible, http://www.desiringgod.org/messages/it-is-right-to-live-for-maximum-pleasure

Chapter 8

Piper's False Gospel

As we contemplate all that has been said in the previous chapters, the unavoidable conclusion is that in Christian Hedonism we are facing not merely a flawed gospel, but a false gospel of John Piper's own making. This final chapter seeks to make that conclusion crystal clear.

The fear of the Lord

Piper's thesis of Christian Hedonism is notable for its indifference to the biblical teaching of the fear of God. In *Desiring God*, to show the things that he thinks God delights in, Piper quotes from Jeremiah: 'I will make with them an everlasting covenant, that I will not turn away from doing good to them.... I will rejoice in doing them good... with all my heart and all my soul (Jeremiah 32.40-41).'[1] But very significant are the words excluded from Piper's quote: 'but I will put my fear in their hearts, that they shall not depart from me'. God will not merely rejoice to do them good, but He will purposely place the fear of God in the hearts of His people so that they shall not depart from Him.

Another example is his use of Psalm 147.11, which he quotes from the ESV: 'The Lord takes pleasure in those who... hope in his steadfast love' (Psalm 147.11).[2] The qualifying phrase, 'fear him', which comes before 'hope', is omitted, and yet is vital to a full understanding of what God is saying in His Word.

It appears that Piper wants to keep the concept of 'the fear of the Lord' away from those he is seeking to persuade to follow his philosophy of hedonism. And here is the reason why—a biblical understanding of the concept will seriously undermine both Piper's hedonism and his antinomianism. Scripture makes it clear. 'The fear of the LORD is the beginning of wisdom: a good understanding have all they that do his commandments: his praise endureth for ever' (Psalm 111.10).

In Psalm 34 King David teaches about the fear of the Lord: 'Come, ye children, hearken unto me: I will teach you the fear of the LORD... Keep thy tongue from evil, and thy lips from speaking guile. Depart from evil, and do good; seek peace, and pursue it' (Psalm 34.11, 13-14). And the book of Proverbs reminds us that: 'The fear of the LORD is the beginning of knowledge: but fools despise wisdom and instruction' (Proverbs 1.7).

The fear of the Lord for the believer is a loving and reverential filial fear, not slavish fear; we gladly accept Him as Creator and Law-giver—the God who has the right to be our Lord, the God whose Word we sincerely seek to obey. We recognise His holy character and worship Him with reverence and godly fear. In the Old Testament a clear connection is made between fearing God, keeping His commandments, loving Him and serving Him. 'And now, Israel, what doth the LORD thy God require of thee, but to fear the LORD thy God, to walk in all his ways, and to love him, and to serve the LORD thy God with all thy heart and with all thy soul, to keep the commandments of the LORD, and his statutes, which I command thee this day for thy good?' (Deuteronomy 10.12-13). To fear God, in a sense, sums up all that is expected of the believer. In Ecclesiastes 12.13 the fear of God is coupled with keeping His commandments and called 'the whole duty of man'. In the Old Testament believers were instructed in this essential biblical truth, which applies equally in the Gospel Age if we mean to walk worthily of our gracious God.

In the New Testament the apostle Paul exhorts believers: 'Having therefore these promises, dearly beloved, let us cleanse ourselves from all filthiness of the flesh and spirit, perfecting holiness in the fear of God' (2 Corinthians 7.1). The fear of God leads to an understanding of God's holy character and a godly fear of the consequences of disobedience. The New Testament adds the extra understanding of our relationship to God as our 'heavenly Father'—we now have a 'filial familiarity' in our reverence. We come as children adopted into His family and we experience the discipline of our heavenly Father. 'My son, despise not thou the chastening of the Lord, nor faint when thou art rebuked of him: For whom the Lord loveth he chasteneth, and scourgeth every son whom he receiveth. If ye endure chastening, God dealeth with you as with sons; for what son is he whom the father chasteneth not?' (Hebrews 12.5-7). Indeed, we may come 'boldly unto the throne of grace'; but we always do so 'with reverence and godly fear: For our God is a consuming fire' (Hebrews 4.16; 12.28-29).

Piper's gospel of easy believism

Piper seems to advocate a gospel of so-called 'easy believism', which means a gospel devoid of convicting recognition of the sinfulness of sin, and the crucial need for repentance unto life. In his book, *The Pleasures of God*, Piper explains, 'the teaching of Scripture is that no one is saved who does not respond to the invitations and commands of the gospel… our response to God is utterly crucial. And God has pleasure in a certain kind of response.'[3] He then comments on the kind of response to the gospel that brings pleasure to God. He writes: 'If the gospel demands a response from sinners, then the demand itself must be good news instead of an added burden, otherwise the gospel would not be gospel.'[4] He then raises the question: 'What kind of command can be Good News?' The answer, he says, is given in Psalm 147.11. 'But the LORD takes pleasure in those who fear him, in those who hope in his steadfast love.' Piper provides this clarification: 'Here we are supposed to fear the one we hope in and hope in the one we fear. What does this mean? I think it means that we should let the experience of hope penetrate and transform the experience of fear. In other words, the kind of fear that we should have toward God is whatever is left of fear when we have a sure hope in the midst of it.'[5] So Piper is promoting the concept of the 'fear of God' as a diminishing commodity that is dissipated by hoping in God. Although here he has acknowledged the fear of God, he has done so in such a way as to effectivly empty it of its real meaning and value.

Piper asserts: 'As a sinner with no righteousness of my own, standing before a self-sufficient and holy God, what command would I rather hear than this: "Hope in my love!".' In our desperate situation, says Piper, God comes to us and says: 'I will save you, and protect you in the storm. But there is a condition… My requirement is that you hope in me.' Piper comments: 'Now I ask, Is this not good news? What could be easier than to hope in God when all else is giving way.

And that is all he requires. That's the gospel.'[6] Piper concludes: 'The beauty of the gospel is that in one simple demand (Put your hope in God) *we* hear good news and *God* gets the glory. That is why God takes pleasure in those who hope in his love—because in this simple act of hope *his grace* is glorified and *sinners* are saved. This is the command of the gospel that keeps God at the center of his affections and ours'[7] (Piper's emphasis).

Piper's view of the gospel is wrong! The message the apostle Paul preached on Mars Hill was that God commands all men everywhere to repent (Acts 17.30). Our Lord said at the commencement of His ministry, 'The time is fulfilled, and the kingdom of God is at hand: repent ye, and believe the gospel' (Mark 1.15).

What Piper has presented to his readers is a false gospel that is without offence; a gospel that is careful to avoid placing any burden on sinners; a gospel that does not call sinners to repentance. It is a classic example of easy believism. Scripture presents a different gospel. On the day of Pentecost, when the apostle Peter preached the gospel, the large gathering responded with deep concern: 'Men and brethren, what shall we do?' Peter said: 'Repent, and be baptized every one of you in the name of Jesus Christ for the remission of sins, and ye shall receive the gift of the Holy Ghost' (Acts 2.37-38). That day three thousand souls were added to the Church. And what is more, verse 43 records that *fear* came upon every soul—believers and unbelievers together felt reverential awe for this holy yet merciful God.

Genuine Christian Joy

At the time of Christ's birth, the angel of God brought this message: 'Fear not: for, behold, I bring you good tidings of great joy, which shall be to all people. For unto you is born this day in the city of David a Saviour, which is Christ the Lord' (Luke 2.10-11). Scripture consistently connects true joy with the proclamation of the gospel, and with the joy that comes from obedience to Christ's commandments. The Lord Jesus said: 'If ye keep my commandments, ye shall abide in my love; even as I have kept my Father's commandments, and abide in his love. These things have I spoken unto you, that my joy might remain in you, and that your joy might be full' (John 15.10-11). Even when they faced persecution 'the disciples were filled with joy, and with the Holy Ghost' (Acts 13.52).

Joy is a spiritual quality that comes from God. True joy is found in knowing and obeying God, and delighting in His glorious attributes and the excellence of His character. To come into His presence through Jesus Christ our Lord, to understand that we are redeemed by the precious blood of Christ, to know sins forgiven and to worship Him as Creator and Saviour is the greatest joy that a human being can experience this side of eternity. Obedience to our heavenly Father's holy commandments brings great joy into the life of the believer. We obey our gracious God because it is right to do so, and because we love Him. So joy is far more than an emotion; it is a fruit of the Holy Spirit.

Even in times of trial and suffering, genuine believers know the joy of God that passes understanding. James, a servant of God, writes to the scattered believers, 'My brethren, count it all joy when ye fall into divers temptations [trials]; knowing this, that the trying of your faith worketh patience' (James 1.2-3).

The apostle Peter encourages believers facing serious trials of faith to rejoice in Jesus Christ: 'Whom having not seen, ye love; in whom, though now ye see him not, yet believing, ye rejoice with joy unspeakable and full of glory: Receiving the end of your faith, even the salvation of your souls' (1 Peter 1.8-9).

As we have seen in previous chapters, John Piper is not speaking of the true Christian joy as taught in Scripture. He is speaking, rather, of the sensual, felt, emotional experience of happiness. And he teaches that Christians should pursue this happiness free of the restraints of God's moral law. There is a world of difference between the genuine joy of the true believer, and the contrived happiness offered by Christian Hedonism.

The Bible distinguishes joy from pleasure. One of the Greek words for pleasure, *hedone*, is the word from which we get our English word *hedonism*. Its use in the Greek New Testament is uniformly negative, denoting gratification of natural or sinful desires.[8] So the word *hedonism*, which describes the philosophy of self-centred pleasure-seeking, is a provocative and inappropriate word to describe the Christian life. Paul referred to 'perilous times' to come when men would be 'lovers of pleasures more than lovers of God' (2 Timothy 3.4). The Bible warns that self-indulgent pleasure-seeking does not lead to happiness and fulfilment. Ecclesiastes 2.1-11 records the sad testimony of the man who sought to build his life on pleasure-seeking. The search left him empty and disillusioned.

The fruit of Christian Hedonism

We see the true face of Christian Hedonism in a typical Passion Conference, as tens of thousands of young people gather together to 'enjoy' a worship experience, led by a large assortment of contemporary 'Christian' worship leaders. Passion 'worship' is characterised by flashing psychedelic strobe lights in a darkened auditorium, thunderous beat music and wild revelry—indeed, the rave ethos of a Passion gathering is indistinguishable from a worldly rock concert. With their minds and emotions deliberately worked up into a state of ecstatic, sensual excitement, the young audience is eager to receive Piper's message—'the vocation of your life is to pursue your pleasure'.[9] But the warning of Scripture could not be clearer: 'Love not the world, neither the things that are in the world. If any man love the world, the love of the Father is not in him. For all that is in the world, the lust of the flesh, and the lust of the eyes, and the pride of life, is not of the Father, but is of the world' (1 John 2.15-16).

Scripture encourages believers: 'But, beloved, remember ye the words which were spoken before of the apostles of our Lord Jesus Christ; how that they told you there should be mockers in the last time, who should walk after their own ungodly lusts. These be they who separate themselves, sensual, having not the Spirit' (Jude 17-19). But Piper's hedonism, together with the Passion movement's ungodly worship, encourages many thousands of young people to walk according to their own ungodly lusts.

The heresy of Christian Hedonism

Having evaluated John Piper's Christian Hedonism in the light of biblical truth, we have uncovered a man-made concept based on an antinomian view of Scripture, a false view of God's love, an ungodly view of worship, a worldly view of happiness, a twisted view of Scripture, and a wrong view of salvation. Over several decades Piper has spent his ministry preaching the flawed doctrines of Christian Hedonism across the USA and in many other countries across the globe, more recently utilising the power of the Internet to do so.

Most alarming is the way he has blatantly distorted and misrepresented Scripture. We must conclude that John Piper's hedonism is a heretical doctrine that presents a false gospel that has no place in the Christian Church. Like all heresies it ultimately destroys those who follow it. It is a doctrine which turns people from the true gospel of salvation in Christ to become pleasure-seekers who indulge in counterfeit worship.

The real challenge of the Christian life is not to 'desire' God and 'enjoy' Him in pseudo-spiritual, hedonistic pleasure. Rather it is to 'walk worthy of the Lord unto all pleasing, being fruitful in every good work, and increasing in the knowledge of God'(Colossians 1.10). We should be on our guard 'lest any man spoil you through philosophy and vain deceit, after the tradition of men, after the rudiments of the world, and not after Christ' (Colossians 2.8).

The message of our Lord is without compromise and easy to understand: 'If any man will come after me, let him deny himself, and take up his cross daily, and follow me' (Luke 9.23). We must strive to keep His Word, and walk even as He walked (1 John 2.5-6). Our faith must express itself in the fruit of the Spirit (Galatians 5.22-23). Our calling in this world is to be 'holy and without blame before Him in love' (Ephesians 1.4), and in the next to serve Him forever (Revelation 22.3-4).

Endnotes

1 *Desiring God*, p53

2 Ibid, p54

3 *The Pleasures of God*, 1991, p202

4 Ibid, p204

5 Ibid, p204

6 Ibid, pp206-207

7 Ibid, p207

8 *Vine's Expository Dictionary*, p861

9 John Piper, Passion address, 'Passion for the Supremacy of God', Part 1, January 2, 1997

Appendix

The Real John Piper in Three Videos

We have produced three videos of John Piper's philosophy of Christian Hedonism that examine his teaching in the light of biblical truth. We believe these videos provide an accurate and fair account of Piper's ministry. By their very nature they are selective, but we have made every effort to be fair in the clips that are presented. Of course, Piper's vast Desiring God network has every opportunity to respond.

Piper's Journey into Hedonism

The first video records his pathway into Christian Hedonism. In his book, *Desiring God*, Piper explains his conversion to Christian Hedonism. During his first quarter in seminary he was introduced to the argument for Christian Hedonism by the writings of Blaise Pascal, who had written: 'All men seek happiness. This is without exception.' This was music to Piper's ears. 'This statement so fit with my own deep longings... that I accepted it and have never found any reason to doubt it.' (*Desiring God*, p19) Henceforth the purpose of Piper's life, as a Christian Hedonist, was to satisfy his own deep longings for happiness and help others do the same.

Piper's 'tremendous longing for happiness' led to 'the growing conviction that praise should be motivated solely by the happiness we find in God...' With the concept of Christian Hedonism firmly implanted in his mind, he turned to the Psalms and 'found the language of Hedonism everywhere.'

https://www.youtube.com/watch?v=NNE2dyrbC30

John Piper in the Dark

The second video focuses on Piper's preaching to the huge Passion Conferences over the past 2 decades. It illustrates Piper's practice of preaching in the dark, and his close association with the contemporary Christian music scene and 'Christian' rap. He has been keynote speaker at many Passion Conferences, delivering his first message, 'Passion for the Supremacy of God', back in 1997. The focus of Piper's address was Christian Hedonism. He asserted that 'God is most glorified in you when you are most satisfied in him… the vocation of your life is to pursue your pleasure. I call it Christian Hedonism.'

A feature of Piper's Passion addresses is that they focus on the philosophy of Christian Hedonism and seldom point young people to the need for repentance of sin.

https://www.youtube.com/watch?v=_QDtKkZDhYk

Folly of Christian Hedonism

The third video, takes a broader look at Piper's hedonistic philosophy. A crucial point is the recognition of Piper's antinomianism. In an interview recorded in 2010 as part of the 'Ask Pastor John' series of podcasts, Piper is asked the straightforward question, 'Are Christians under the Ten Commandments?' His response is unequivocal: 'No. The Bible says we're not under the law.' In his address to Passion 2017 Piper boldly declares that disobedience to God's law and law-breaking is not the ultimate essence of evil. He extols the overwhelming importance of Christian Hedonism as a way of life. 'Christian Hedonism is not a game. It is what the whole universe is about. The radical implication is that pursuing pleasure in God is our highest calling.' Piper says to his young audience: 'Disobedience to the command of God is not more basic, not more fundamental, not more ultimate than what they [Adam and Eve] desired above God.' But Piper's interpretation of the sin of Adam and Eve is wrong and misleading, as we seek to show.

https://www.youtube.com/watch?v=yzNoQwrZkdg

The above vidoes are available for viewing on our website:
www.therealjohnpiper.com

Made in the USA
Middletown, DE
12 November 2017